D0535051

How to Use This Book

Look for these special features in this book:

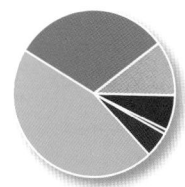

SIDEBARS, **CHARTS**, **GRAPHS**, and original **MAPS** expand your understanding of what's being discussed—and also make useful sources for classroom reports.

FAQs answer common **F**requently **A**sked **Q**uestions about people, places, and things.

WOW FACTORS offer "Who knew?" facts to keep you thinking.

TRAVEL GUIDE gives you tips on exploring the state—either in person or right from your chair!

PROJECT ROOM provides fun ideas for school assignments and incredible research projects. Plus, there's a guide to primary sources—what they are and how to cite them.

Please note: All statistics are as up-to-date as possible at the time of publication.

Consultants: Karen Egan, LSTA Grants Consultant, Illinois State Library; William Loren Katz; William W. Shilts, PhD, Chief of the Illinois State Geological Survey

Book production by The Design Lab

Library of Congress Cataloging-in-Publication Data
Burgan, Michael.
  Illinois / by Michael Burgan.
      p. cm.—(America the beautiful, Third series)
  Includes bibliographical references and index.
  ISBN-13: 978-0-531-18559-9
  ISBN-10: 0-531-18559-1
  1. Illinois—Juvenile literature. I. Title. II. Series.
  F541.3.B87 2008
  977.3—dc22   2006036020

1 2 3 4 5 6 7 8 9 10 R 16 15 14 13 12 11 10 09 08

AMERICA ★ THE ★ BEAUTIFUL

Illinois

BY MICHAEL BURGAN

Third Series

Children's Press®
A Division of Scholastic Inc.
New York ★ Toronto ★ London ★ Auckland ★ Sydney
Mexico City ★ New Delhi ★ Hong Kong
Danbury, Connecticut

CONTENTS

GROWTH AND CHANGE

Illinois farmland drew new settlers, and Chicago shined during the World's Columbian Exposition . . **38**

4

MORE MODERN TIMES

One of the richest states in the country felt the blow of the Depression and contributed to the U.S. effort in several wars. It changed during the civil rights movement, and today, the future points to new challenges **56**

5

9 TRAVEL GUIDE

Stroll through the Windy City, explore an unspoiled forest, or catch a game at Wrigley Field . . **104**

PROJECT ROOM

★

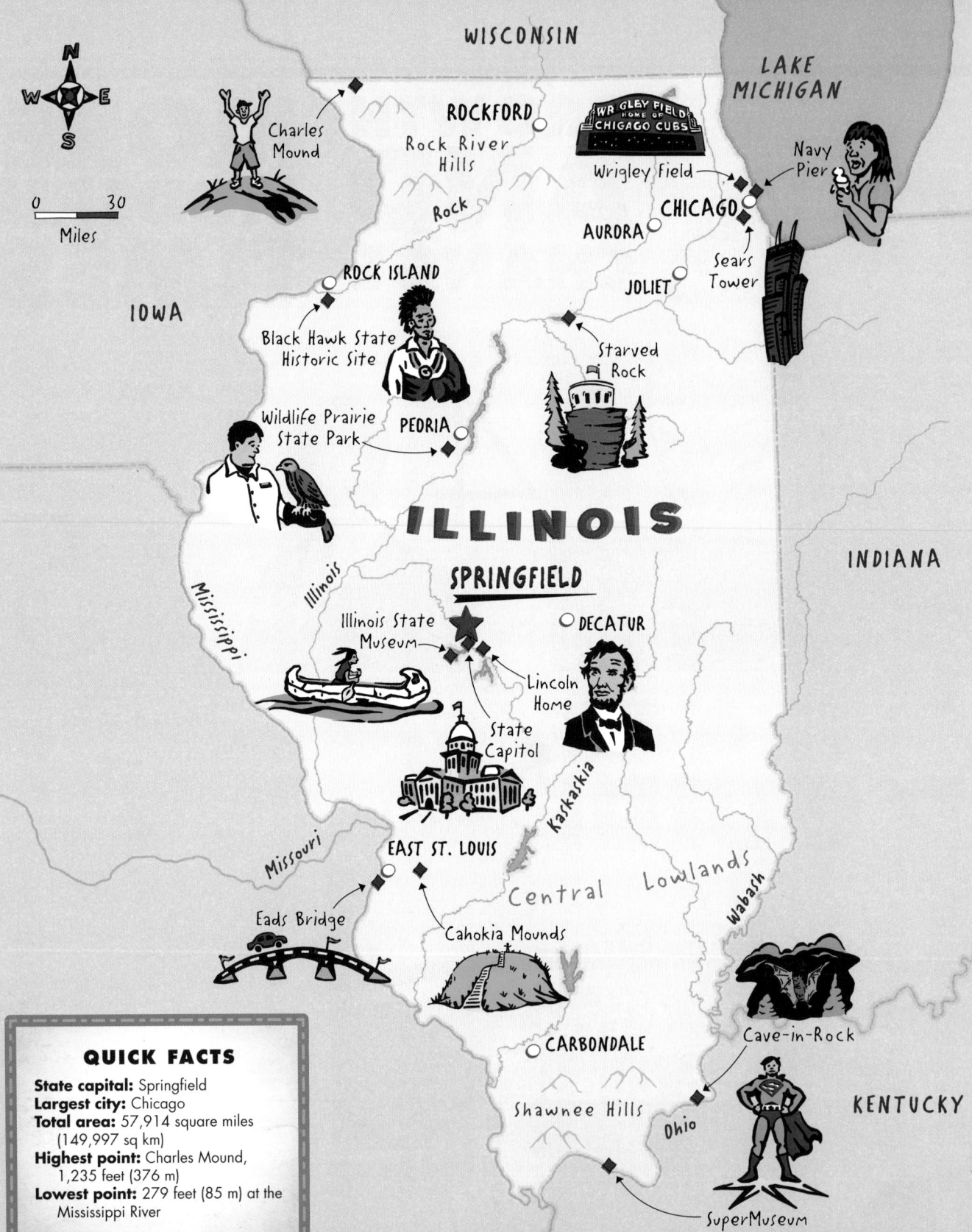

WISCONSIN

LAKE MICHIGAN

N W E S

0 30 Miles

Charles Mound

ROCKFORD

Rock River Hills

Rock

WR GLEY FIELD HOME OF CHIGAGO CUBS

Wrigley Field

Navy Pier

CHICAGO

AURORA

Sears Tower

JOLIET

IOWA

ROCK ISLAND

Black Hawk State Historic Site

PEORIA

Wildlife Prairie State Park

Starved Rock

ILLINOIS

Illinois

SPRINGFIELD

Mississippi

Illinois State Museum

DECATUR

Lincoln Home

State Capitol

INDIANA

Kaskaskia

Missouri

EAST ST. LOUIS

Central Lowlands

Wabash

Eads Bridge

Cahokia Mounds

Cave-in-Rock

CARBONDALE

Shawnee Hills

Ohio

KENTUCKY

SuperMuseum

Welcome to Illinois!

HOW DID ILLINOIS GET ITS NAME?

It was hundreds of years ago, in 1673. And French-Canadian explorers had sailed southwest across Lake Michigan and into unfamiliar lands. They met a Native American group that called itself the Illiniwek. What did that mean? It was an Algonquian word for "the men" or "tribe of superior men." The French spelled the group's name *Illinois* and first used the word to name a river that ran through Illiniwek lands. Before long, it was used to name the land itself. To the French and other Europeans who followed, the Illinois country meant the region between the Mississippi River and the Ohio River. And now, historians agree, that's how the state of Illinois got its name!

8

READ ABOUT

Lush, fertile
farmland is plentiful
throughout the
central and southern
regions of Illinois.

CHAPTER ONE

LAND

★

WHAT WILL YOU FIND IN ILLINOIS? Beautiful prairies, farms, and rolling hills, but that's just the beginning. The state is the 25th largest, and its 57,914 square miles (149,997 square kilometers) are home to a wide variety of plants and animals. But it is not a land of extremes. Its highest point, at Charles Mound, is just 1,235 feet (376 meters). And its lowest spot rests along the Mississippi River at 279 feet (85 m).

AN ICY PAST

What's the source of that rich Illinois soil? Ice and wind! Tens of thousands of years ago, Earth went through several ice ages. During these periods, large sheets of ice called glaciers moved southward from the Arctic region. Some glaciers were several thousand feet thick! Between 300,000 and 125,000 years ago, a glacier now called the Illinoian covered large parts of North America. In Illinois, it reached as far south as the modern city of Carbondale. As the temperature warmed, the glacier **receded**. Perhaps 12,000 to 25,000 years ago, the Wisconsinan glacier covered the northern third of the state. Only small parts of northwestern and southern Illinois escaped the icy grip of these two glaciers.

As the glaciers receded, they flattened the ground. They also left behind sand and minerals. Some of these deposits gave Illinois its rich soil.

Low areas in the land hollowed out by the glaciers filled with water to become lakes. Many important rivers eroded deep and wide valleys in the glacial deposits. Continuing floods along these rivers also have helped to enrich the soil in the floodplains. The flooding of the Mississippi and Illinois rivers left behind deposits that made the land perfect for growing crops. One agricultural region is called the American Bottom.

WORD TO KNOW

receded *pulled or moved back over time*

Illinois Geo-Facts

Along with the state's geographical highlights, this chart ranks Illinois's land, water, and total area compared to all other states.

Total area; rank	57,914 square miles (149,997 sq km); 25th
Land; rank	55,584 square miles (143,962 sq km); 24th
Water; rank	2,331 square miles (6,037 sq km); 20th
Inland water	756 square miles (1,958 sq km); 28th
Great Lakes	1,575 square miles (4,079 sq km); 6th
Geographic center	In Logan County, 28 miles (45 km) northeast of Springfield
Latitude	36° 58′ N to 42° 30′ N
Longitude	87° 30′ W to 91° 30′ W
Highest point	Charles Mound, 1,235 feet (376 m)
Lowest point	279 feet (85 m) at the Mississippi River
Largest city	Chicago
Number of counties	102
Longest river	Illinois River, 273 miles (439 km)

Source: U.S. Census Bureau

Illinois is the **25th-largest state in total area**, putting it right in the middle of the list. Alaska, the largest state, is almost 12 times bigger than Illinois.

LAND REGIONS

The state of Illinois is bordered by the Mississippi River on the west. On the other side of that river are Iowa and Missouri. To the north is Wisconsin, and to the east is Indiana. The Wabash and Ohio rivers mark the state's boundaries on the southeast and south. And this is where Kentucky is located.

The landscape can be grouped into four main regions: the Driftless Area, Central Plains, the Shawnee Hills, and the Gulf Coastal Plain.

FAQ

Q8 WHAT IS THE AMERICAN BOTTOM?

A8 *Bottom* is an old-fashioned word for low-lying land near a river. The American Bottom refers to the land south and east of where the Mississippi, Illinois, and Missouri rivers meet. It covers 175 square miles (453 sq km).

Illinois Topography

Use the color-coded elevation chart to see on the map Illinois's high points (orange) and low points (green to dark green). Elevation is measured as the distance above or below sea level.

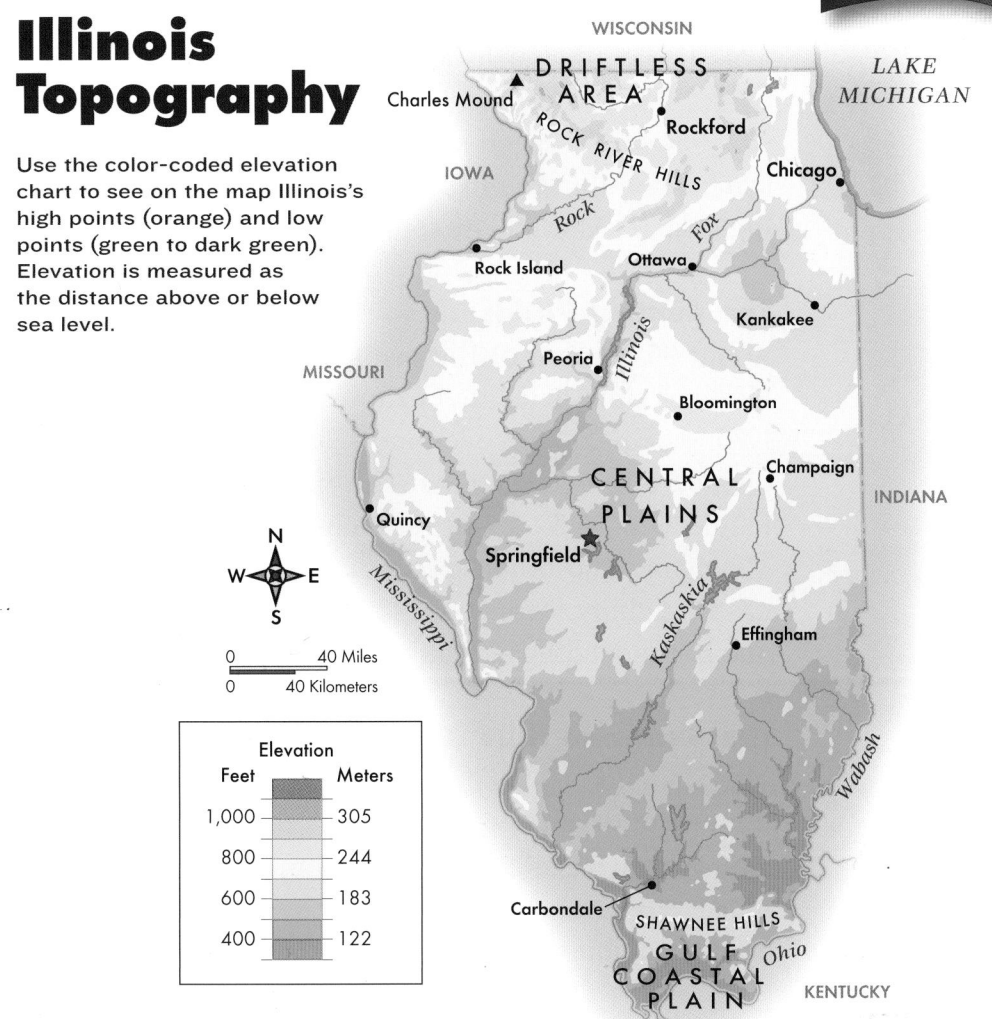

| Elevation | |
Feet	Meters
1,000	305
800	244
600	183
400	122

The Central Plains region is known as the Heart of Illinois and is characterized by its small towns, rolling hills, and flourishing agriculture.

The Driftless Area

This area in the northwest corner of the state was never covered by glacial ice. The area has deep valleys and steeper, more rugged hills than much of the rest of the state. Several of the highest points in the state, including Charles Mound, are found here.

The Central Plains

About 90 percent of Illinois is covered by the Central Plains region. This area extends west and south from Lake Michigan to cover most of the state. It can be divided into two sections. The first is the Great Lakes Plain, which is a low stretch of land along Lake Michigan. The other section is the Till Plains, which has incredibly fertile soil. This rich soil makes Illinois one of the leading agricultural states in the nation.

The Shawnee Hills

The Shawnee Hills stretch across the southern part of Illinois south of the Central Plains. This narrow strip of land is from 5 to 40 miles (8 to 64 km) wide and about 70 miles (113 km) long. Like the Driftless Area, it is marked by rugged, forested hills and deep valleys.

The Gulf Coastal Plain

This area is located at the extreme southern tip of Illinois. It is covered by the northernmost edge of the Coastal Plain that stretches north from the Gulf of Mexico. The land here has gentle slopes and is swampy in many places. The bald cypress and tupelo gum trees that grow in the swamps make this part of Illinois resemble parts of the Deep South.

WEATHER AND CLIMATE

At about 390 miles (628 km) long, Illinois stretches out over a long area—about the distance from Cape Cod, Massachusetts, to Virginia. Just as that area along the eastern seaboard has widely varying climates, so does Illinois. Warm winds from the Gulf of Mexico keep the southern half generally warmer and wetter than the northern half. Snowfall is scarce in the south. Cairo, at the southern tip of the state, averages only 10 inches (25 centimeters) of snow per year, while spots in the north near Lake Michigan average almost 40 inches (102 cm) per year.

Other factors affect the weather in Illinois. There are no mountains near the western edge of the state. So huge thunderstorms can roll across the Great Plains and barrel into Illinois. Some of the largest storms pack powerful tornadoes, which have often brought heavy damage to Illinois.

Weather Report

117°F **-36°F**

This chart shows record temperatures (high and low) for the state, as well as average temperatures (July and January) and average annual precipitation.

Record high temperature . . . . 117°F (47°C)
    at East St. Louis on July 14, 1954
Record low temperature . . . . –36°F (–38°C)
    at Congerville on January 5, 1999
Average July temperature . . . . 73°F (23°C)
Average January temperature . . . . 22°F (–6°C)
Average yearly precipitation . . . . 36.3 in. (92.2 cm)

Source: National Climatic Data Center, NESDIS, NOAA, U.S. Dept. of Commerce

THE TRISTATE TORNADO

Cutting through the middle of the United States is a region called Tornado Alley. The states in the "alley" see more twisters than any other part of the country. And they have been hit by some of the most damaging storms. Southern and central Illinois sit along the eastern edge of Tornado Alley. In 1925, the deadliest U.S. tornado ever (perhaps a series of tornadoes) ripped through the southern part of the state on its way from Missouri to Indiana. The path of the 1925 TriState Tornado was 219 miles (352 km) long, and the twister lasted for three and a half hours. Two towns were especially hard hit: Murphysboro, where more than 200 people died, and De Soto, where 69 people, mostly children, were killed at a school.

On Lake Michigan, severe winds and changes in air pressure can create huge waves called seiches. A seiche that hit Chicago in 1954 was 10 feet (3 m) tall!

Illinois National Park Areas

This map shows two Illinois areas protected by the National Park Service.

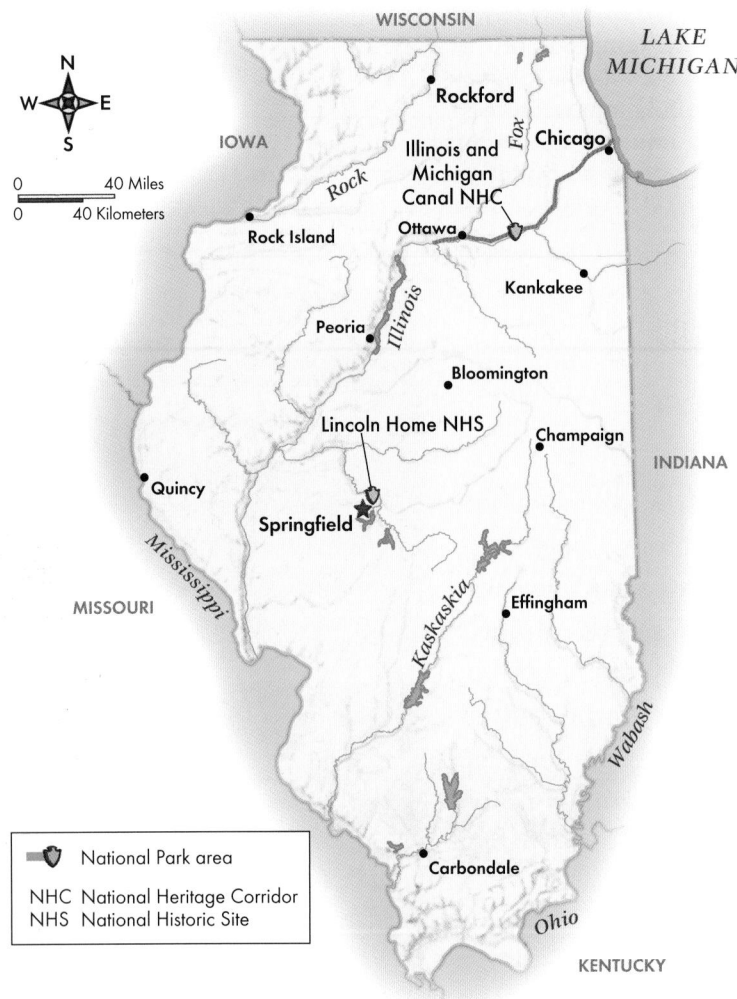

National Park area

NHC National Heritage Corridor
NHS National Historic Site

The area around Lake Michigan has its own climate. In the summer, winds off the lake help keep the shore cooler than the middle part of the state. In winter, the water temperature is usually warmer than the air, so the lake breezes help keep Chicago and other shoreline towns warmer than the interior. The winds can also bring lake-effect snows. Cold winds that stream down from the Arctic can suck up moisture from the lake and produce snow.

FLOODS

Illinois's rivers have helped make the soil rich and fertile. They have also helped people move goods more easily. But from time to time, the rivers go wild, flooding their banks and destroying property. The worst flood to hit the state came in 1993, after months of heavy rain caused the Mississippi to flood. Across the Midwest, about 50 people died, and tens of thousands had to flee their homes. In Chester, Illinois, the floodwaters reached a height of 22.7 feet (7 m) above the flood stage height, shattering the previous record by more than 6 feet (1.8 m). The flooding there came in two distinct waves. The city was flooded for a total of 186 days!

ANIMAL LIFE

Over thousands of years, a variety of animals have adapted to the varying conditions in Illinois. The state is home to more than 500 kinds of mammals, birds, and fish, as well as almost 100 species of reptiles and amphibians. Forests are home to the white-tailed deer, as well as raccoons, foxes, and squirrels. Look to the sky and you might spot bald eagles and golden eagles. More common birds are cardinals, blue jays, and several kinds of ducks and owls. The bluegill and other kinds of sunfish, trout, bass, and catfish can be found in the state's streams and lakes.

PLANT LIFE

Illinois's prairies used to be covered with prairie grass and forests. Today, most of the prairies have been plowed under to make farmland, but some 2,500 native plant species remain. These include different types of prairie clover and sunflowers, black-eyed Susans, wild onions, and various grasses. The state's forests also boast trees such as oak, sugar maple, beech, ash, hickory, and walnut. They provide welcome shade in the summer, and colorful backgrounds when their leaves turn each fall. One Illinois tree found only in the southern part of the state is the bald cypress. It thrives in the swampy lands of that region.

HUMANS AND THE ENVIRONMENT

The loss of Illinois's prairie is just one sign of the effect humans have had on the land. Today, state residents wrestle with a number of environmental problems.

ENDANGERED ANIMALS

Illinois is working hard to protect animals that are endangered. These are species that could die out if their homes and food supplies are not preserved. Among the endangered birds in Illinois are the piping plover, least bittern, short-eared owl, little blue heron, and snowy egret. Some endangered fish include the cypress minnow, sturgeon, and northern brook lamprey. Endangered bats in Illinois include the gray bat and Indiana bat.

A little blue heron

WOW

Humans have shaped the shoreline of Lake Michigan. In Chicago, they put dirt in the lake, then held it in place with stone blocks weighing up to 8 tons.

If the Asian carp ever entered the Great Lakes, it would probably become the dominant fish and disrupt the food chain.

WORD TO KNOW

invasive species *wildlife that is not native to a region and harms native plants or animals*

Across Illinois, they are trying to preserve the wildflowers and grasses that remain on what was once open prairie. The state encourages citizens to plant their own prairie gardens.

Invasive species are another environmental concern. Invasive species include nonnative wildlife that has been introduced to a region where it harms native plants or animals. One example is the Asian carp. This 4-foot-long (1.2-m) fish can weigh up to 100 pounds (45 kilograms), a sign of its healthy appetite. The carp was brought to the United States during the 1970s to eat algae in ponds where catfish are raised. Floods carried the carp out of the ponds and into nearby rivers. The carp reached the Illinois River and could eventually enter the Great Lakes. If they do, they will eat the food that native fish need to survive. The U.S. government is building a barrier near Chicago to keep the carp out of Lake Michigan.

MINI-BIO

PAT CHARLEBOIS: SAVING THE WATERS

Want to learn about the Asian carp? Ask Pat Charlebois (1966–). As a scientist with the Illinois Natural History Survey, she studies the carp and other invasive sea life that threaten the health of Illinois's rivers and the Great Lakes. In addition to the carp, other harmful creatures include the zebra mussel and the round goby. Charlebois educates the public, including Illinois students, about the problem of invasive species. She says, "Children pass on their knowledge to adults and tuck away that knowledge for use into their adulthood."

? Want to know more? See www.iisgcp.org/aboutus/staff/patkristin.htm

Air pollution is also a concern in Illinois. Coal burned to fuel electrical power plants in Illinois and other states releases mercury and other harmful substances into the air. In 2006, a leading Illinois power company agreed to install equipment that will reduce the amount of these substances it releases. Some Illinois power plants are investigating the use of wind power as an alternative to burning coal. And the Illinois State Geological Survey is developing ways of capturing mercury from the gases of coal-fired power plants, and it is leading studies on ways to capture and permanently store the carbon dioxide that forms when coal is burned to make electricity.

Another sign of environmental health came in 2006. After years of restoring wetlands in the state, residents saw their first nesting wild trumpeter swans in more than 150 years. The majestic 4-foot-tall (1.2-m) waterbirds were once common in the state, but were almost wiped out by hunters. The Lincoln Park Zoo in Chicago raised some of the swans in captivity, then released them into the wild.

The trumpeter swan is the largest waterfowl in North America.

READ ABOUT

This is a replica of a wooly mammoth. Prehistoric people in Illinois hunted these animals for food and clothing.

c. 10,000 BCE

First humans follow large game to the region

c. 2000 BCE

Native Americans begin building villages

▲ c. 200 BCE

The Hopewell settle in Illinois

FIRST PEOPLE

★

WITH THE END OF THE LAST ICE AGE IN ILLINOIS, PREHISTORIC ANIMALS BEGAN TO ROAM THE PRAIRIE. They included mastodons and mammoths—early relatives of today's elephant. These and other mammals sometimes came to salty springs in southern Illinois. Starting around 10,000 BCE, humans followed these mammals into the region.

860 CE

Mississippians move into the area

1150

The Cahokia community has as many as 20,000 people

1500s ►

The Illiniwek move into Illinois

ILLINOIS'S FIRST SETTLERS

The first settlers to arrive in what we know as Illinois hunted the animals for food. They also made tools from the animals' bones and wore their skins and furs for clothing. The first settlers lived in caves or under overhanging rocks. They tracked their game as the animals moved across the area. At times, the first residents of Illinois also fished and gathered nuts, berries, and seeds to round out their diet. Ancient bones found in Greene County show that early Illinoisans also kept dogs as pets.

BUILDING COMMUNITIES

Life for the first Native people of Illinois began to change around 2000 BCE. Much of the big game they had once hunted was now extinct. The people turned to smaller wild animals for food or relied more on plants. The people also began building the first villages, usually near waterways. They made clay pots and stone tools, and remains of these items help **archaeologists** understand how the early Illinoisans lived.

By around 200 BCE, people now called the Hopewell settled in Illinois and much of the Midwest. The Hopewell had great skills. They made art out of clay, mica, shells, and copper. And they traded their goods over a wide area, from the Rocky Mountains to the Atlantic coast. Their crops included corn, squash, pumpkins, and beans.

WORD TO KNOW

archaeologists *scientists who study the items left behind by ancient peoples*

Hopewell settlements featured dome-shaped homes called wigwams. These homes had wooden frames covered with animal skins, tree bark, or mats made from plants.

Native American Peoples

(Before European Contact)

This map shows the general area of Native American peoples before European settlers arrived.

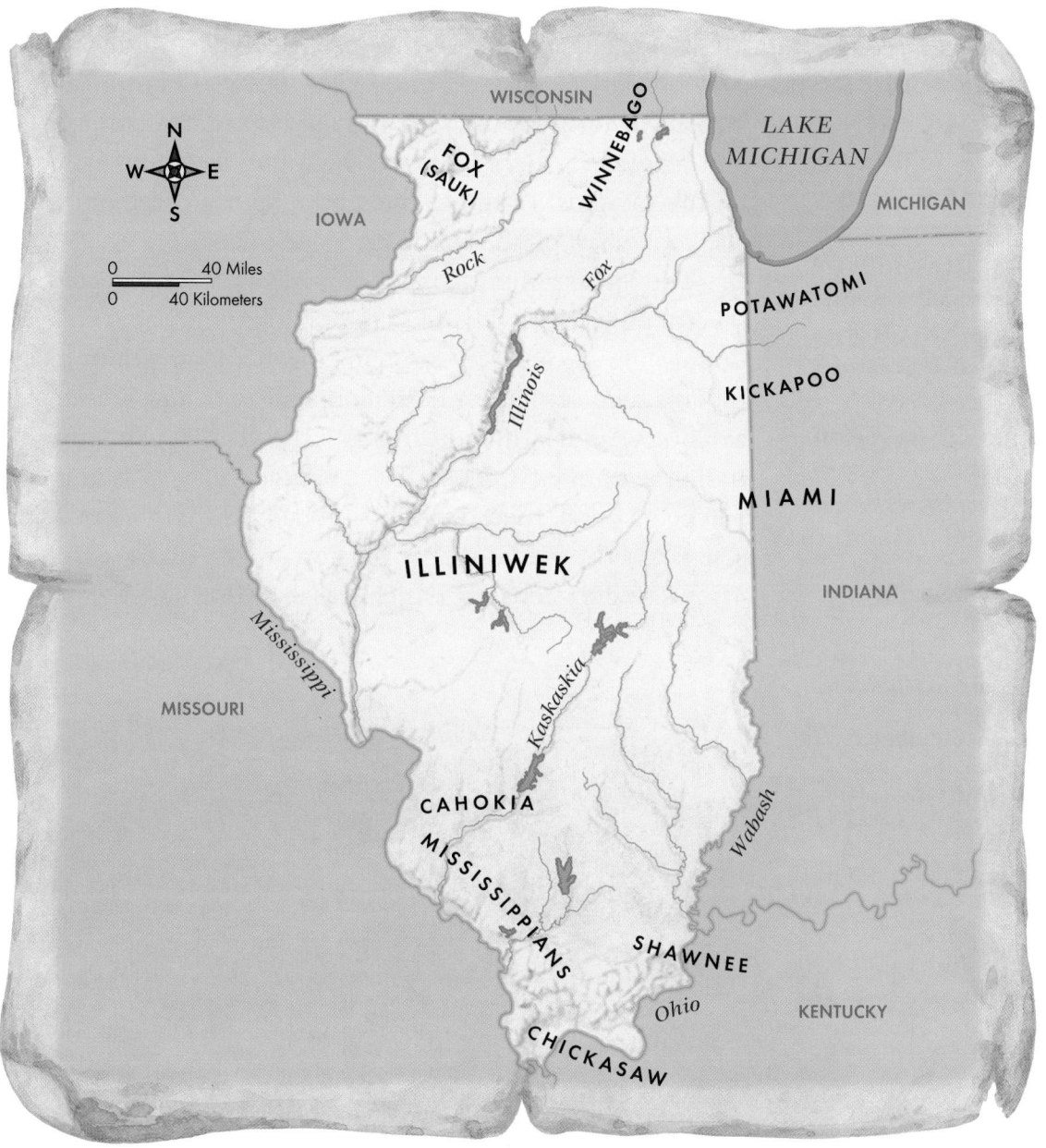

SEE IT HERE!

THE CAHOKIA MOUNDS STATE HISTORIC SITE

Want to see the view the Great Sun saw from his home in Cahokia? Head to Cahokia Mounds State Historic Site in Collinsville. You can climb to the top of the Great Sun's mound, now called Monks Mound. From there, you can see other remaining mounds and the grand plaza, an open space in the center of the former city. The Cahokia Mounds site has been named a World Heritage Site, honoring its historical importance.

WOW

The highest mound in Cahokia was about the height of a modern five-story building! It was reserved for the most powerful chief, who was called Great Sun.

The Cahokia Mounds, the largest prehistoric structures in Ilinois

THE GREATEST MOUND BUILDERS

For some unknown reason, around 500 CE, the Hopewell and their culture disappeared from the Midwest. Within a few hundred years, however, Mound Builders moved into the region from the Southeast. Known as the Mississippians, they built the greatest Indian culture in North America. Some mounds were 100 feet (30 m) high, but only a few were used for burials. Instead, the political and religious leaders lived the "high life" in homes built on the mounds. Public events and religious ceremonies also took place on these human-made hills.

The largest Mississippian city was Cahokia, located several miles east of the Mississippi River in what is now Collinsville, Illinois. It was named for a later group of Indians who settled in the region shortly before French explorers came to Illinois. In about the year 700, the first Indian settlers of Cahokia built simple villages. Within 150 years or so, the Mississippians moved into the area. They raised large amounts of crops, particularly corn. They also grew tobacco, which was used during religious

ceremonies. In Cahokia, the Mississippians built more than 120 mounds, made from countless basketfuls of dirt hauled by workers to the site.

At its peak around 1150, Cahokia was a bustling city with as many as 20,000 people. No other city in North America had as large a population until 1800, when Philadelphia hit that mark. Surrounding Cahokia was a wooden wall some 15 feet (4.6 m) tall, meant to keep out enemies. The city also had a giant wooden calendar, often called "Woodhenge" today. This giant sun calendar built by the Mississippians was made from large wooden posts placed in a circle in the ground. Between 900 and 1100, as many as five of these circles were built.

Inside the city, skilled workers made tools, jewelry, and religious objects. Other residents ventured outside the wall to hunt and fish. Smaller villages arose outside Cahokia. Their residents headed to the city for religious events and public gatherings.

THE RISE OF THE ILLINIWEK

Like the Hopewell, the Mississippians eventually disappeared. Cahokia was abandoned in about 1400. Soon, other Native American tribes entered Illinois. In the early 1500s, the Illiniwek moved from Michigan and into Illinois. As the century went on, they spread west and as far south as Arkansas. The Illiniwek spoke an Algonquian language and were not just one group but rather a **confederation** of Indian nations. Individual tribes included the Cahokia, Kaskaskia, Michigamea, Moingwena, Peoria, and Tamaroa. The confederation had one main chief, while each individual nation had its own subchiefs.

Most Illiniwek villages were established where the soil was best—in the American Bottom and along the

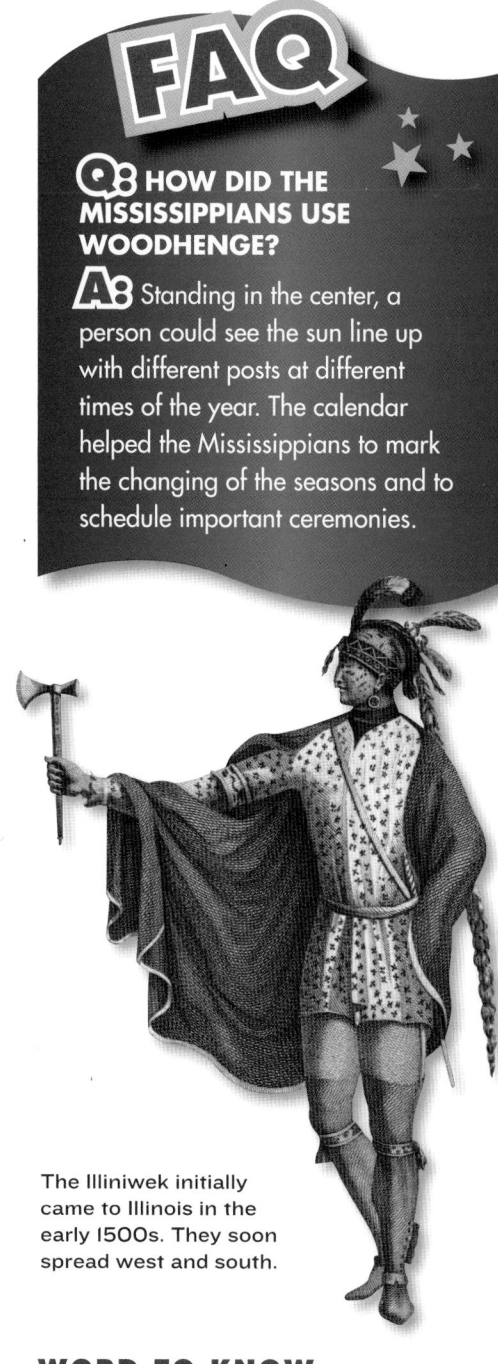

FAQ

Q8 HOW DID THE MISSISSIPPIANS USE WOODHENGE?

A8 Standing in the center, a person could see the sun line up with different posts at different times of the year. The calendar helped the Mississippians to mark the changing of the seasons and to schedule important ceremonies.

The Illiniwek initially came to Illinois in the early 1500s. They soon spread west and south.

WORD TO KNOW

confederation *a union of several political or social groups*

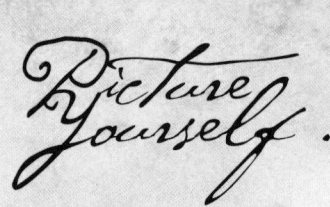

Picture Yourself . . .

in an Illiniwek Village

If you were one of the Illiniwek children, you began working at an early age. You would help the women plant crops and gather nuts and berries. If you were a girl, you'd spend more time with your mother as you got older and would learn farming skills. If you were a boy, you would spend time with your father. As a teenager, you would have to prove your talent as a hunter. Once you did that, you could marry. All teenagers were sent out alone into the woods for a spiritual event called a vision quest.

But life wouldn't be all work and no play. You would have toys such as tops and dolls, and you could play lots of games. You could also watch your parents at play. Illiniwek men played lacrosse, a ball-and-stick game invented by Native Americans. Illiniwek women enjoyed a game that used dice.

Illinois River. The Illiniwek spent part of the year in fixed villages, another part of the year hunting, and the winter months in scattered camps. Women were the farmers, planting corn, beans, squash, and other crops in the spring. Men hunted turkey, deer, elk, and smaller animals such as raccoons. They also fished, traveling the rivers in boats called pirogues. To make these boats, the men set fire to large logs, then scraped away the charred remains to create a hollow spot where they could sit. In the summer, everyone worked together to hunt bison. After the hunt, women harvested crops and tanned bison hides while the men preserved the meat for the coming winter.

The men of the Illiniwek nations were primarily hunters and warriors. They often fought with neighboring tribes, such as the Sauk and the Fox. At times, the various tribes of the region raided one another's villages to capture people to use as slaves.

The Illiniwek and neighboring tribes could stop a war by showing a special pipe called a calumet. The wooden stem of the calumet was decorated with colored feathers and the heads and necks of birds. Ceremonies that featured one person dancing in a circle while holding this tobacco pipe strengthened peaceful ties between tribes.

In their everyday lives, the Illiniwek believed they were surrounded by spirits. Some spirits were good and could help them kill game or ensure a good harvest. Other spirits were evil, causing sickness and accidents. The Illiniwek also believed in one supreme spirit, Kitchesmanetoa, who had created the universe. The universe, the Illiniwek believed, included an underworld where monsters lived.

One of these monsters was painted on rocks along the Mississippi River. The beast had claws and horns, red eyes, a long tail, and a human face.

The Illiniwek turned to religious figures called **shamans** to help them win the support of good spirits and weaken the evil ones. Shamans were thought to have the power to enter the spirit world and predict the future. They were also doctors, using both their spiritual powers and herbal medicine to cure the sick.

By about 1650, as many as 13,000 Illiniwek lived in Illinois. Around this time, however, they faced an invasion from the Iroquois Confederation from New York. The Iroquois were skilled warriors with one powerful advantage—guns from European traders. The arrival of the Iroquois led some Illiniwek to move west to Iowa and Missouri. But as Europeans began coming to Illinois during the 1660s, some Illiniwek returned to the eastern side of the Mississippi River.

WORD TO KNOW

shamans *spiritual leaders who had powers to cure the sick and influence events*

MINI-BIO

D. ANTHONY TYEEME CLARK: NATIVE AMERICAN SCHOLAR

At the University of Illinois, D. Anthony Tyeeme Clark (1964–) shares his knowledge of Native Americans with eager students of all backgrounds. He is a citizen of the Meskwaki First Nation. Meskwaki is the Algonquian name for the people known in English as the Fox. Clark has written about historic Native American struggles against white American settlers. He has also taken a strong stand against sports teams using Indian names and symbols.

? Want to know more? See www.nah.uiuc.edu/faculty-Clark.htm

26

READ ABOUT

In the 1600s,
fur traders from
Canada came to
what is now Illinois.

▲ **1673**
*Louis Jolliet and Father
Jacques Marquette
explore the region*

1680
*René-Robert Cavelier,
Sieur de La Salle,
leads an expedition
into Illinois*

1703
*The French found
a settlement called
Kaskaskia*

CHAPTER THREE

EXPLORATION AND SETTLEMENT

★

T HE ILLINIWEK SAW THEIR LIVES BEGIN TO CHANGE DURING THE 1660s AND 1670s. Suddenly, there were strange men coming down the rivers that ran through Native lands. Some sought furs. Some wore long, black robes. And almost all of them spoke a foreign language. The strangers were French fur traders and priests. They came from Canada to make contact with the Illiniwek and neighboring tribes.

1720

The first enslaved Africans reach the region

1763

The British win the French and Indian War

1779 ▲

Jean-Baptiste Pointe du Sable settles in what is now Chicago

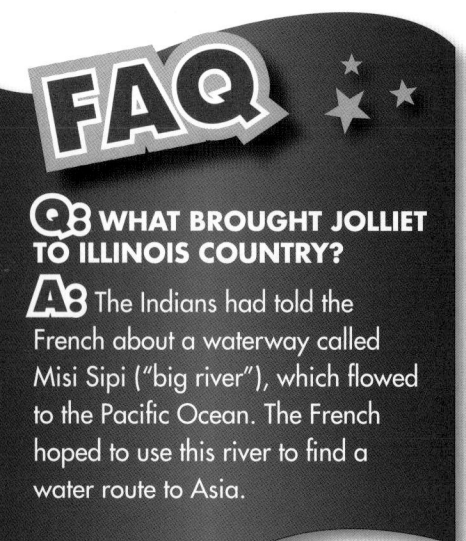

FAQ ★ ★ ★

Q8 WHAT BROUGHT JOLLIET TO ILLINOIS COUNTRY?

A8 The Indians had told the French about a waterway called Misi Sipi ("big river"), which flowed to the Pacific Ocean. The French hoped to use this river to find a water route to Asia.

EUROPEANS ARRIVE

At the time, France was one of several European nations exploring and settling North America. Since the 1500s, the French, Spanish, English, and others had braved long, difficult voyages across the Atlantic. They wanted to claim land in North America for themselves. They would control the natural resources they found and then bring them back to Europe. One valuable resource was beaver fur. Europeans used it for coats and hats. Indian trappers brought the furs to white traders, who then shipped the furs to Europe. The Europeans also set up governments in their new lands similar to the ones they had in Europe.

Louis Jolliet and Father Jacques Marquette kept detailed accounts of their travels through Illinois.

Trappers and Missionaries

In 1671, the French claimed the Illinois country. The first detailed European account of the tribes of the region came from the 1673 expedition led by an experienced French Canadian fur trapper named Louis Jolliet. Traveling with him was Father Jacques Marquette, a Roman Catholic **missionary**. Sailing from Canada with a crew of white and black men on oars, the expedition crossed Lake Michigan. Jolliet and Marquette then followed the Fox and Wisconsin rivers to the Mississippi River. The explorers reached present-day Arkansas before heading back to Canada. On the return trip, they cut across Illinois on the Illinois River.

Both Jolliet and Marquette kept detailed journals of their trip, but only Marquette's survives. He described meeting an armed tribe that seemed ready to attack the Frenchmen. But in reality, "what we took for a signal for battle was an invitation [for] . . . us to draw near, that they might give us food." Later in the journey, Marquette started a mission among the Kaskaskia Indians, but it was eventually destroyed by the Iroquois. The French founded another mission along Lake Michigan, at what is now Chicago. That one failed, too, though some French traders and trappers remained in the region.

MINI-BIO

JACQUES MARQUETTE: MISSIONARY AND EXPLORER

A Roman Catholic priest, Father Jacques Marquette (1637–1675) arrived in Canada from France in 1666. His goal was to convert North American Indians to the Roman Catholic faith, the official religion of France. After learning several Algonquian languages, Marquette was chosen to go with Louis Jolliet to explore the Mississippi River. On the way back to Canada, Marquette and Jolliet met the Illiniwek. Marquette became ill on this return trip. He stayed in Wisconsin before returning to Illinois in 1675. He died later that year in Michigan.

WORD TO KNOW

missionary *a priest, minister, or other deeply religious person who tries to convince others to practice a certain religion*

European Exploration of Illinois

The colored arrows on this map show the routes taken by explorers between 1673 and 1682.

A Growing French Presence

In 1680, an expedition led by René-Robert Cavelier, Sieur de La Salle, entered Illinois from the east and found Africans, probably escaped slaves, living among the Shawnee. La Salle and his men sailed along the Kankakee River to the Illinois River. Near present-day Peoria, they built the first European fort in Illinois. The fort, however, was soon destroyed. So La Salle built a second fort, called Starved Rock, on a high spot along the Illinois.

A third French fort, Fort Pimitoui, was the largest of them all. It was built by Henri de Tonti, an Italian soldier who had come with La Salle to Illinois. He wore an iron hook to replace a hand he had lost in

Starved Rock State Park gets its name from a Native American legend about a band of Illiniwek who were under siege and starved at the top of the bluff.

French traders did business and sometimes also socialized with the Native Americans.

battle. Indians brought furs to Tonti at Fort Pimitoui and exchanged them for metal goods and cloth. The French then shipped the furs to Canada and eventually to Europe. Fort Pimitoui also had a mission and several small buildings inside its high, wooden walls.

For the most part, the Indians of Illinois got along well with the French. Indian women married French traders, and the two peoples blended their cultures. The French learned to eat Native American food and wear traditional clothing. And many of the Indians became Roman Catholics. Even before the French arrived, the Illiniwek had traded with other Indians for European goods, such as weapons, knives, and household items. With the arrival of the French, they had easier access to these goods.

The native people preferred dealing with the French over the British, another major group of traders and settlers. The French did not try to grab all the Indians' land for themselves as the British did. The Illiniwek also welcomed the French traders' willingness to live with them and try to learn their ways. Still, the Illiniwek faced hardships as the decades went on. Illnesses brought by the Europeans killed thousands of them; so did wars with other tribes. Many Indians pushed westward to avoid these problems. By 1700, only about 6,000 Native Americans remained in Illinois, and the number fell to less than 1,000 just 50 years later.

One of the remaining Native American groups in the northern region was the Fox, and they sometimes battled the French. The problems with the Fox led the French to shift their trade to the south, in the American Bottom. In 1703, they founded a settlement called Kaskaskia, along the Mississippi River. It became the major French town in colonial Illinois. Other notable settlements nearby included Cahokia, Prairie du Roche, and Fort de Chartres.

Unlike Great Britain, France limited immigration to its colonies in North America. So the towns in southern Illinois remained small. Some of the settlers were Europeans who served as **mercenaries** in the French army.

SLAVERY IN ILLINOIS

The first enslaved people from Africa reached the region in about 1720. About 500 were brought to work in mines and later were sold to local families. In general, though, slaves in French lands had more legal rights and protections than slaves in English colonies. Owners were expected to make sure slaves were fed and clothed, and a number of slaves were eventually given their freedom.

During the 19th century, flooding forced the people of Kaskaskia to flee their hometown. All that remains of the original site today is a small island in the Mississippi River.

WORD TO KNOW

mercenaries *soldiers who will fight for any army willing to pay them*

The Mississippi and Kaskaskia rivers meet at this spot. The French settled in this region and called their settlement Kaskaskia.

Picture Yourself...

on the Frontier

The Illinois frontier of the 18th century blended the cultures of three peoples: French, Indian, and African. If you were a child from any of those groups, you were expected to do chores on the farm. And if you got any formal learning, it took place at home, not in schools. Children born to an Indian mother and a French father were considered French citizens. But they could follow either parent's culture. Girls as young as 12 were considered old enough to marry. Boys over 12 were allowed to carry guns, yet they were not legally considered adults until they were 25. By law, enslaved children remained with their mothers at least until they were 12.

WORD TO KNOW

allies *friends or supporters, especially during wartime*

FRENCH RULE

By the 1750s, the population in French-controlled Illinois was fewer than 2,000, including enslaved people. Although they lived far from major cities, the residents of Illinois had plenty of food and could easily trade for goods. This was possible because of the many waterways in the region. Despite their small numbers, the French settlers of Illinois produced grain that was sold in other French lands, especially Louisiana to the south. Other goods, such as meat and leather, were also shipped down the Mississippi River and sold abroad.

THE BRITISH ARRIVAL

In 1763, a war fought beyond the Illinois frontier brought great changes to the region. For decades, France and Great Britain had been battling to control the fur trade and settlement of North America. The British won this battle with their victory in the French and Indian War (1754–1763). This was a war that the British fought against the French and their Native American **allies**. With this success, the British gained almost all of France's colonies east of the Mississippi River. In 1765, the British arrived at Fort de Chartres to take control of

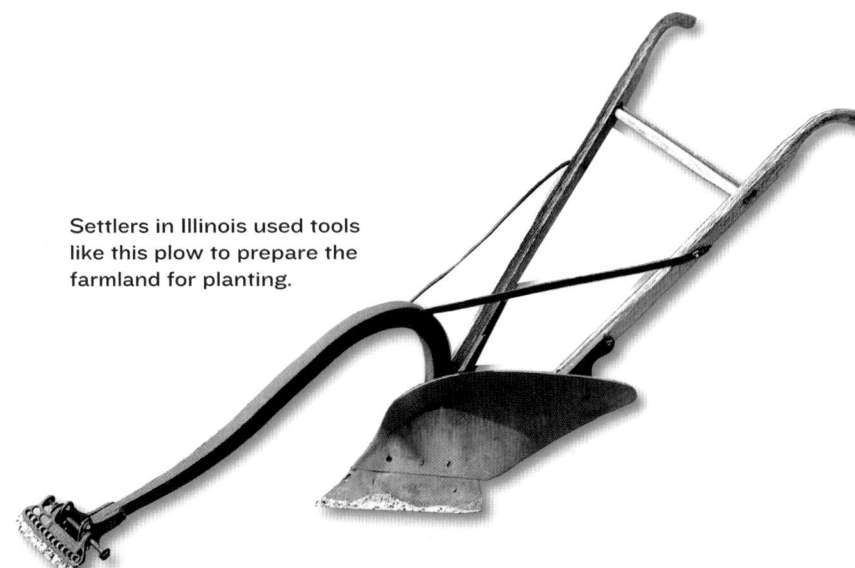

Settlers in Illinois used tools like this plow to prepare the farmland for planting.

Early settlers in Illinois lived in simple cabins. They cleared land and planted corn and other crops.

the Illinois country. Many French settlers crossed to the west side of the Mississippi River to avoid British rule. The British assured those who stayed that they would "enjoy the same rights and privileges, the same security for their persons and effects" as they had before.

In 1766, British army captain Harry Gordon recorded some of his impressions of the new British colony of Illinois: "In the route we pass le Petit Village . . . a place formerly inhabited by 12 families now only by one since our possession. The abandoned houses are most of them well built and left in good order, the grounds are favorable near the village for grain, particularly wheat; and extensive cleared land, sufficient for the labor of 100 men to [farm]. . . . [At Cahokia] here are 43 families of French who live well. . . . There are likewise 20 cabins of Peoria Indians left here."

SEE IT HERE!

FORT DE CHARTRES

The original Fort de Chartres was a simple wooden building surrounded by a moat. In 1753, the French built a much larger and stronger fort out of huge limestone blocks, but when the British took control of Illinois, they let most of Fort de Chartres crumble. In the 20th century, the state of Illinois took over the land and rebuilt the fort. The oldest building in Illinois, it is now a state historic site.

JEAN-BAPTISTE POINTE DU SABLE: SUCCESSFUL TRADER

In 1779, a free African trader named Jean-Baptiste Pointe du Sable (1745–1818) put down roots in Chicago. He was born on the Caribbean island of Hispaniola (today, that's the Dominican Republic and Haiti). Du Sable was the first permanent, non-Indian resident of modern Chicago. He settled on the Chicago River, set up a trading post, and married Catherine, a Potawatomi woman. The family entertained such famous frontier figures as Daniel Boone and Chief Pontiac. Today, the city's museum of African American history bears du Sable's name, and the U.S. Postal Service has issued a stamp celebrating Chicago's first citizen.

? Want to know more? See www.dusablemuseum.org/

For the next decade, few British came to Illinois. The British wanted its colonists along the Atlantic coast to stay east of the Appalachian Mountains. The colonists would be easier to control there, and they would not spark wars with the Indians of the Midwest by seizing their lands. In 1774, the British made Illinois part of Quebec—France's former colony in Canada. And they once again promised to protect the rights of the French settlers.

WINNING ILLINOIS

The next year, tensions between American colonists and Great Britain erupted into war, starting the American Revolution (1775–1783). For three years, the fighting was well to the east of Illinois, but it finally arrived in 1778. A Virginian named George Rogers Clark had a bold plan to attack the British fort in Detroit. His first step was to take control of the Illinois country. He led about 175 men to Kaskaskia. The French residents there gave him the fort before he fired a shot. Clark then took over Cahokia and several other villages and won the support of local Indian tribes. Some of the French joined Clark as he headed east to capture the British fort at Vincennes, along the Wabash River.

Through the winter of 1778–1779, the Americans and their allies trudged through near-freezing swamps to reach Fort Sackworth in Vincennes. Once

Troops under the command of George Rogers Clark cross the Wabash River. They went on to seize Vincennes from the British.

again, Clark was victorious. Americans remained in the Illinois country for the rest of the war, and Illinois became part of Virginia. Later in 1779, Bellefontaine became the first permanent Illinois town founded by American settlers.

The American Revolution ended in 1783, and the United States grew to include all the British lands east of the Mississippi River. Four years later, Illinois became part of the Northwest Territory. This region stretched west of the Ohio River to the Mississippi. Handfuls of settlers came to Illinois. But to most Americans, the land beyond the Ohio and Wabash rivers still seemed like a foreign country.

READ ABOUT

The journey to
Illinois was long
and difficult.
Settlers packed
their belongings
in wagons and
headed west.

1795
*Native Americans sign
the Treaty of Greenville*

▲**1818**
*Illinois becomes
a state*

▲**1832**
*The Black Hawk
War is fought*

CHAPTER FOUR

GROWTH AND CHANGE

★

S OME RODE IN WAGONS OVER ROCKY, BUMPY TRAILS. Many more poled flat-boats down the Wabash and Ohio rivers. Americans began to work their way westward into Illinois, arriving in small numbers. There, they found Native American villages, French families, and some British traders.

1848

The Illinois and Michigan Canal is completed

▲ **1871**

Chicago suffers a devastating fire

1905

Robert Abbott founds the Chicago Defender

BATTLE FOR TERRITORY

In time, the Americans from the East would outnumber Native Americans and early European settlers. But it took several decades after the American Revolution—and more warfare—for this to happen.

By the 1780s, the Potawatomi, Miami, Kickapoo, and other groups had settled near Illinois, in the Northwest Territory. Some, such as the Potawatomi, had battled American settlers during the last years of the American Revolution. After the war, these groups sometimes attacked towns in the Northwest Territory. The Indians did not want the settlers taking their lands. These raids convinced some Americans that the frontier was a dangerous place.

In response to their land being taken away from them, Native Americans sometimes raided settlers' communities and farms.

By the early 1790s, the conflict between the Native Americans and settlers had turned into a war. The Indians believed they had been tricked out of their lands, and they wanted to reclaim all the territory north of the Ohio River. The U.S. government rejected this. In 1794, General "Mad Anthony" Wayne won a major victory against Indian forces in Ohio. With that defeat, the Native Americans agreed to give up their claim to most of Ohio. The next year, they signed the Treaty of Greenville. This agreement also required them to turn over land in Illinois, including the sites of Chicago and Peoria.

MINI-BIO

BLACK HAWK: BATTLE LEADER

The Black Hawk War of 1832 was named for Black Hawk (1767–1838), a Sauk chief who led his people in a battle to reclaim their ancestral lands in Illinois. Despite the Treaty of Greenville, peace did not truly come to the frontier until this war was fought. Black Hawk formed an Indian confederation to challenge the Americans, but his forces were greatly outnumbered. The battle resulted in 70 settlers and soldiers losing their lives. Hundreds of Black Hawk's men were killed.

THE COMING OF THE SETTLERS

The Treaty of Greenville helped increase American settlement in Ohio and Indiana, but newcomers were still unsure about Illinois. Those who did venture there clung to the southern rivers and the towns already established along them, such as Cahokia and Kaskaskia. A few hardier souls set off into the forests to look for clearings where they could build log cabins and plant corn. Most of the early American settlers came from southern states, such as the Carolinas, Kentucky, and Tennessee. Few ventured north to the prairies, thinking that the treeless land could not produce crops.

The early settlers' cabins were simple, with dirt floors. And the newcomers often used hunting knives to eat their dinner.

Illinois: From Territory to Statehood
(1809–1818)

This map shows the original Illinois territory and the area (outlined in red) that became the state of Illinois in 1818.

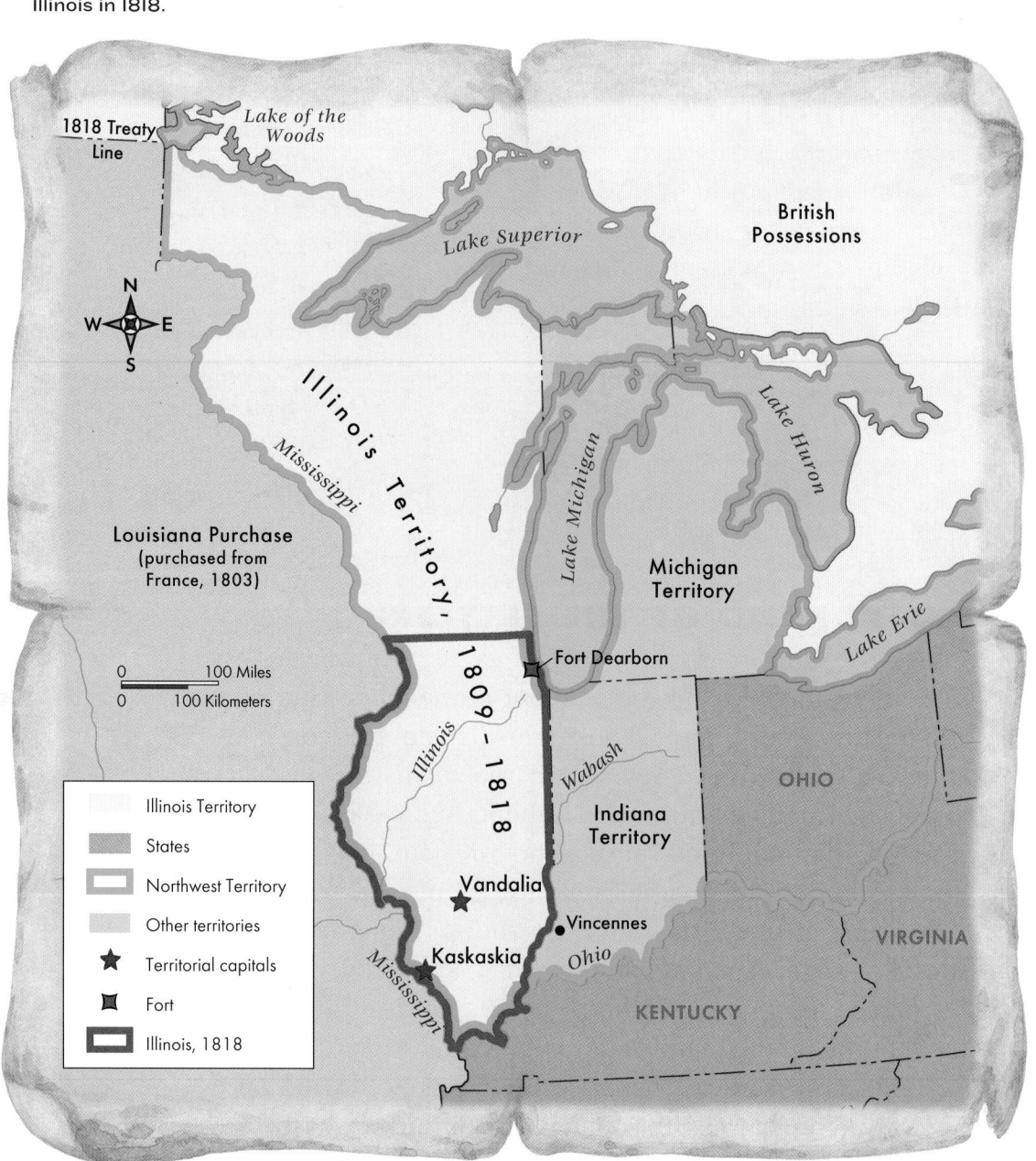

Fort Dearborn on the Chicago River in 1812. This was the site of a battle between U.S. troops and Indian allies of the British.

As late as 1834, one Illinois resident said even the richest farmer "lives in a house not half so good as [an] . . . old hog pen, and not any larger." Those simple homes did not keep the settlers very warm, and the settlers battled a range of diseases, such as malaria and typhoid.

At first, buying land from the U.S. government wasn't easy. The government wanted to settle old legal battles over who owned what land before selling more. Finally, by the late 1810s, the problems were settled, and more land was put up for sale. The government also set aside land in western Illinois, called the Military Tract, for soldiers who had fought in the War of 1812 against Great Britain. During the war, in August 1812, Indian allies of the British attacked Americans leaving Fort Dearborn, a U.S. Army post in Chicago. Sixty men, two women, and twelve children were killed.

The mechanical reaper, invented by Cyrus McCormick, was pulled by horses.

GROWTH IN THE NORTH

In 1819, Illinois became a state, and residents decided to move their capital from Kaskaskia to a new city, Vandalia. (Springfield became the capital in 1837.) As more people arrived, many headed for towns looking for work. Some went to Shawneetown, by the mouth of the Wabash River. The area had salt mines, where African American slaves did the hard work of digging out the valuable mineral. White settlers came to set up stores, banks, and other businesses. At the opposite end of the state, in Galena, workers mined for lead, and businesses also sprang up in that region.

During the 1830s and 1840s, more of the new settlers in Illinois came from New England and other parts of the Northeast. Part of the draw was the farmland of the prairies. In 1837, John Deere, a recent arrival in Illinois, made a cast-steel plow that could easily rip through the hard prairie. Underneath, farmers learned, was some of the richest soil in the world. Another important invention was Cyrus McCormick's reaper. The machine could cut wheat much faster than a farmer could by hand. Deere set up a factory in Moline, and McCormick moved his reaper business to Chicago in 1847.

Joining the new American settlers in Illinois were European immigrants. Before 1860, most came from Germany and Ireland. The Germans tended to be farmers and business owners. The Irish found work mining in Galena and building railroads and canals. By 1850, some 38,000 Germans were scattered across the state, and almost 28,000 Irish called Illinois home. In addition, there were settlers from France and Canada, as well as some African Americans who had fled slavery or arrived as free men and women soon after the American Revolution.

A large percentage of the Irish went to Chicago, which had become the major city of the Midwest. The boom there started during the 1830s, after Americans had signed a treaty with the Potawatomi and other area tribes. The Indians agreed to swap their land around Lake Michigan for settlements farther west. American settlement in Chicago increased as plans were made to build a canal from Lake Michigan to the Illinois River. The Illinois and Michigan Canal was completed in 1848. And it allowed ships to sail from New York through the Erie Canal, across the Great Lakes, and then down the Mississippi.

By the mid-1800s, Chicago had become a bustling city. A center for trade, it relied on its railroad and ports.

Between 1850 and 1860, the rail system in Illinois grew to serve the entire state. The railways were instrumental in the development of the region, allowing farm produce, mineral ore, and coal to be transported with ease. When the Illinois Central Railroad was completed in 1856, it stretched from Cairo to Galena, with a route to Chicago as well. At 705 miles (1,135 km), it was the world's longest rail line at the time.

Chicago became a center for trade in the Midwest, and its importance only grew in the decades to come. In 1857, Gustaf Unonius, a Finnish visitor to Chicago, gave this description of the city: "The growth of the city during the last sixteen years seems almost miraculous—even for America." From 1840 to 1860, Chicago's population boomed from 4,470 people to more than 112,000!

SLAVERY AND THE CIVIL WAR

Illinois citizens were deeply divided over human bondage. Though the Northwest **Ordinance** of 1787 made slavery illegal in the Illinois territory, slaveholders brought in Africans as indentured servants. (These are people who sign up to work for others for a specific amount of time, in return for being taken care of but not paid.) This failed. Then they tried to deny people of color a right to enter Illinois, and that failed. When Illinois joined the Union, its legislature passed laws that kept blacks from voting, holding public office, testifying in court, and serving in the militia. Not until 1845 did the Illinois supreme court rule that indenture was an illegal form of slavery.

Occasionally, free blacks in Illinois were kidnapped and sent to work as slaves in the South. Still, some Illinoisans were **abolitionists**, such as Alton newspaper publisher Elijah Lovejoy. In 1837, he was killed by a proslavery mob that opposed his views.

By 1858, Illinois had produced two important national political figures. Stephen A. Douglas was a noted senator who wanted to become president of the United States. Abraham Lincoln was an attorney who challenged Douglas for his Senate seat. Though Lincoln lost the election, his forceful

WORDS TO KNOW

ordinance *a law passed by local governments*

abolitionists *people who were opposed to slavery and worked to end it*

ELIJAH LOVEJOY: BRAVE ABOLITIONIST

In 1836, editor Elijah Lovejoy (1802–1837) arrived in Alton and began to publish his antislavery newspaper, the *Observer*. Its circulation soon rose to 1,500 copies. The next year, a proslavery white mob destroyed Lovejoy's press. He bravely imported another press. "If I fall, my grave shall be made in Alton," announced the determined Lovejoy. But another mob attacked the *Observer*, killed Lovejoy, and destroyed the press. Lovejoy became the first important white person to die fighting against slavery and for freedom of the press. Later his brother Owen, who tried to help him protect his press from the mobs, was elected to Congress.

LAND OF LINCOLN

Illinois is called the "Land of Lincoln"—Abraham Lincoln, that is. Born in Kentucky in 1809, Lincoln spent most of his adult life in Illinois. Today, the state has several historical sites that honor the former president. New Salem features a reconstruction of the buildings that stood when Lincoln called the town home during the 1830s. In Springfield, visitors can walk the same floors Lincoln did in his former home, the place where he lived while running for president. Lincoln is buried in the city's Oak Ridge Cemetery.

WORD TO KNOW

Industrial Revolution *the rapid growth of factories and use of large machines to produce goods that began in England in the 18th century*

arguments opposing slavery's expansion won many followers and national attention. Lincoln knew slavery was wrong and that prohibiting its expansion westward would lead to its eventual death.

Lincoln knew how slavery pitted the North against the South. And he had warned that the country "cannot endure, permanently, half slave and half free." Yet when he ran for president in 1860, Lincoln promised the South he would not end slavery if he were elected, and he meant it. He would just stop its growth. Lincoln won the election, but the Southern states did not believe his promise. In 1861, 11 slave states seceded from the Union, sparking the Civil War.

As a Northern state, Illinois sent troops to fight for the Union. A total of 259,092 Illinoisans served in the Union army, including 1,811 African Americans. But support for the South and its cause was strong in the southern half of the state. Illinois officials shut down newspapers there that opposed the war and arrested people who openly supported the South. Still, on the whole, Illinois played an important role for the Union. Mound City, on the Ohio River, was the site of a naval shipyard. And Confederate prisoners were kept on Rock Island in the Mississippi River just west of Moline. Illinois was also the home of the most important Union general of the war, Ulysses S. Grant, who later became president of the United States.

THE BIRTH OF AN INDUSTRIAL GIANT

With the Union victory in 1865, Illinois was ready to grow again. Factories were sprouting up all across the United States. This was part of the **Industrial Revolution** sweeping large parts of the world. Manufacturing became an even larger part of the Illinois economy,

Boats and buildings aflame during the Great Fire of 1871. The blaze spread quickly through Chicago and left 90,000 people homeless.

THE GREAT CHICAGO FIRE

On the night of October 8, 1871, smoke began to fill the sky over Chicago. A fire started near DeKoven Street on the west side of the Chicago River and soon spread over an area 4 miles (6.4 km) long and 1 mile (1.6 km) wide. Families moved from street to street, hoping to outrun the advancing flames. Firefighters had a difficult time controlling the massive blaze which burned for nearly 30 hours. Rainfall finally helped put the fire out.

Aftermath

When it was over, flames had destroyed more than 73 miles (117 km) of road, 120 miles (193 km) of sidewalk, 2,000 lampposts, 17,500 buildings, and $222 million in property. Of Chicago's 300,000 residents, 90,000 were left homeless and nearly 300 had died. But the city quickly went to work to rebuild. And by 1875, little evidence remained of the fire.

and the state remained a center for shipping goods to and receiving goods from all over the nation. Chicago overcame a devastating fire in 1871 to continue its role as the economic engine for the state. The city was the center for meatpacking, as hogs and, later, cattle were brought there to be killed and butchered for dinner tables across the country. By the early 20th century, Chicago was known as the "hog butcher to the world."

Of the many people who helped make Chicago a sprawling meat market, two stand out. Gustavus Swift, a butcher from Massachusetts, reached Chicago in 1875. He created a system that carried the dead cattle and hogs through the factory on a moving chain. Workers could get the meat without having to move for it. In 1881, Swift also built the first successful refrigerated railroad cars, so his meat could be safely shipped across the country. Like Swift, Philip Armour used machinery to move his animals through the factory. Armour also built

George Pullman used fine materials to create comfortable cars that surrounded passengers in luxury.

a fleet of refrigerated cars even larger than Swift's. The two men did not want to waste any of their animals, so they used some parts to make products such as leather, soap, and glue. It was said that the Chicago meat men used "everything but the squeal."

Like the "meat men" Swift and Armour, George Pullman helped make Chicago a 19th-century industrial giant. Pullman came to Chicago in 1859 and soon perfected the sleeping car, which ended the uncomfortable ride many passengers faced on long train trips. His Pullman cars used the finest woods and fabrics, so riders rode in luxury. The cars were staffed by servants, recently freed African American slaves, who were called Pullman porters. Just south of Chicago, Pullman started his own town, named for himself, where he built a factory and homes for his workers.

The city and the surrounding area also became an important center for making steel and furniture and was the birthplace of shopping by mail. Montgomery Ward and Sears, Roebuck & Co. shipped out catalogs across the United States. Families in remote parts of the country could order goods—including carriages and even house-building kits!—that they could not find in local stores. The railroads that traveled through Chicago then carried the goods to waiting customers. The trains ran on coal, which powered their steam engines. Coal was also used in steel mills and to heat homes. Illinois had large deposits of coal. And coal mining became an important industry in the southern half of the state.

By the late 1800s, Chicago had much to celebrate. So it was a huge honor for the city to hold the World's Columbian Exposition. This event, also known as the Chicago World's Fair, celebrated the 400-year anniversary of Christopher Columbus's arrival in the Americas. The opening ceremonies were held in 1892, but the grounds weren't opened to the public until May 1893.

This fair showcased the arts, architecture, and the American spirit. The first Ferris wheel was introduced at the Columbian Exposition, and Buffalo Bill Cody's Wild West show was a huge attraction. Chicago proved to the world that it had recovered from the fire of 1871.

The Ferris wheel was the creation of George Ferris. It made its debut at the World's Columbian Exposition in Chicago in 1893.

WORDS TO KNOW

unions *organizations formed by workers to try to improve working conditions and wages*

strike *to refuse to work, as a sign of protest*

MAY DAY

In the 1880s, Chicago gave birth to many new American trade **unions**. Union members were appalled at the harsh, unsafe conditions and low pay they faced in factories. And there were long hours: as many as 12 hours a day, six days a week. Many women and children suffered under worse conditions and were paid even less than male workers. Laborers had no vacations, sick leave, or unemployment insurance. The city's wealthiest industrialists and bankers did not want to raise wages, reduce working hours, or make the changes that would protect people on the job. They hated the new unions.

But workers were determined to better their conditions. On Saturday, May 1, 1886, almost 200,000 American men and women across the country stopped work to **strike** for the day. Many marched in the world's first May Day parade. Chicago, the hub of the union movement, had the largest parade: 80,000 people. Two of its strongest leaders were Albert Parsons, a printer and radical union organizer, and his wife, Lucy Gonzalez Parsons, an African-Indian-Spanish woman who had been a slave. They and their two children led people down Michigan Avenue, calling for the eight-hour workday.

May Day in Chicago was bright and sunny. Marchers wore their best Sunday clothes, brought their families, and joked a lot. But the city's leading bankers and industrialists looked at the march and saw the face of revolution. Newspapers predicted violence, so police were everywhere, and armed National Guard troops stood ready. But in Chicago and across the country, May Day was a peaceful day.

On that day in 1886, Illinois had created an important global holiday. By 1890, men and women marched

in every large European and American city. In later years, U.S. union leaders instead decided to celebrate their own "Labor Day" in September.

Meatpacking houses were a common sight in cities such as Chicago and Rockford, as Illinois was the center of the meatpacking industry.

A FLOOD OF IMMIGRANTS

By 1900, Chicago had a population of 1.7 million, making it the second-largest city in the United States. Chicago was also home to more than 35 percent of the entire state's residents. Most of the growth in the city was fueled by immigrants. They came to the United States with hopes of a better life. During the 1890s, more than 500,000 immigrants settled in Chicago, and thousands more went to other cities, such as Rockford and Peoria. The immigrants were increasingly coming from Southern and Eastern Europe: Poland, Russia, the Czech Republic, Hungary, Slovakia, Lithuania, Greece, and Italy.

Although many of these immigrants found jobs in the stockyards and steel mills, the pay was low, the hours were long, and conditions were harsh and dangerous. In addition, the new immigrants often faced **prejudice**. Starting in the 1880s, some people tried to make life easier for

WORD TO KNOW

prejudice *an unreasonable hatred or fear of others*

JANE ADDAMS: FIGHTING FOR RIGHTS

Born in Cedarville, Jane Addams (1860–1935) went to college in Rockford. She worked in England before moving to Chicago and opening Hull-House. Her work did more than help immigrants. She fought for the first juvenile courts in the nation, supported the right of women to vote, and promoted the interest of workers who joined unions. In 1931, she won the Nobel Peace Prize, making her the first U.S. woman to receive that honor.

Want to know more? See http://www.uic.edu/jaddams/hull/newdesign/ja.html

the immigrants and others who lived in crowded city neighborhoods. In 1889, Jane Addams opened Hull-House in Chicago to teach immigrants English and help them find jobs. Other cities soon had "settlement houses" modeled after Hull-House.

The Civil War had ended slavery, but newly freed slaves often found it hard to make a living on the farms of the South. Starting in the 1890s, many black families headed north to industrial cities, looking for work, and many came to Illinois and Chicago in particular. One notable African American who settled in Chicago was Ida B. Wells-Barnett. Her writings told the world about the horrors of lynchings, the illegal hanging of blacks by whites. Another important black journalist in Chicago was Robert Abbott. In 1905, he founded the *Chicago Defender*. It became one of the leading African American newspapers in the United States. Abbott urged more Southern blacks to join the Great Migration

MANY WAYS TO WORK

As the Industrial Revolution went on, some Illinoisans chose not to work in factories. Since these were the days before refrigerators, folks relied on huge blocks of ice to keep food cold. Some of that ice was "harvested" from the Illinois River. Workers cut the blocks of ice using saws. The river also provided mussels and clams. Fishers wanted them for their shells, which were used to make buttons. One job that was unique to Chicago was making harps. The modern harp was invented there in 1889, as skilled workers perfected a design that came from Europe. Today, Chicago remains the harp-making capital of the world.

out of the South. The largest wave of new arrivals hit Chicago in 1910. Tens of thousands left southern states, where they had few opportunities for owning land or making money. They were eager to get city jobs and experience the excitement of urban life. During the next decade, the city's African American population soared, going from 44,000 to 110,000.

FIGHTING A WORLD WAR

In 1917, President Woodrow Wilson led the United States into World War I, which had begun in Europe in 1914, to "make the world safe for democracy." Once again, Illinoisans did their part. About 315,000 of them served in the military during the war. In 1904, the U.S. Navy opened its largest training base along Lake Michigan, just north of Chicago. Many pilots, flying the first war-planes, also trained at two airfields in the state.

The war ended in November 1918 with a victory for the United States and its allies. Cheering crowds in Illinois welcomed the returning soldiers. The people of the state looked ahead to what they hoped would be a bright future.

Many pilots tested the first Sopwith F-I Camel fighter planes taking off from Illinois airfields.

READ ABOUT

Officials inspect cattle at the Chicago Stockyards in the early 1900s.

1920s
Louis Armstrong plays in Chicago nightclubs

1945
Manuel Perez Jr. fights in World War II

◄1959
Jesse Jackson first comes to Illinois

CHAPTER FIVE

MORE MODERN TIMES

★

DURING THE 1920S, ILLINOIS WAS HUMMING. Great music flowed from nightclubs. And in cities such as Chicago, Peoria, Moline, Decatur, and Joliet, factories turned out farm equipment, processed foods, and electrical equipment, while mills produced iron and steel. The state was also a top agricultural producer: farmers grew large amounts of corn and soybeans, and they raised cattle and hogs.

◄ **1973**
The Sears Tower is finished

1983 ►
Harold Washington becomes mayor of Chicago

2007
Chicago chosen as U.S. Olympic Committee selection for 2016 Olympics

58

MINI-BIO

WILLA BEATRICE BROWN: EARLY FLYER

Willa Beatrice Brown (1906–1992) was the first female African American to earn a commercial pilot's license. Brown learned to fly in Chicago in the 1930s, and she married her instructor, Cornelius R. Coffey. Together they opened the Coffey School of Aeronautics, which trained African Americans to become pilots and airplane mechanics. Brown led the battle to integrate the Army Air Corps (now called the U.S. Air Force). When she finally won that struggle, her Chicago school was chosen to train black pilots who fought during World War II.

THE ROARING TWENTIES

Illinoisans deepened their love of the automobile. By 1930, the state had one of the most modern systems of paved roads in the United States. Chicago's position in the middle of the country made it an early center for a new type of transportation as well: the airplane.

The 1920s are sometimes called the Roaring Twenties. The U.S. economy was strong, and Americans entertained themselves like never before. Talented musicians such as Louis Armstrong came to Chicago to play and record jazz music.

Meanwhile, in sports, University of Illinois football player Red Grange became a national sports hero. But there was a dark side to the happy times. The 18th Amendment to the Constitution made drinking alcohol illegal, so criminals turned to bootlegging—illegally importing or making and selling alcohol. Chicago was one of the centers of bootlegging and organized crime. The Federal Bureau of Investigation (FBI) worked with local officials to fight the crime that often troubled the city.

A TOUGH TIME FOR EVERYONE

The 1920s ended when the United States entered the Great Depression, the worst economic period in its history. By October 1931, more than 1 million people were out of work just in Illinois. That was about 15 percent of the state's population. Chicago-area factories

Hard times fell beyond Chicago's city limits as well. Here a family on relief is living in a shantytown in Herrin.

slashed their workforces. And many coal mines in the southern part of the state shut completely. Ben Isaacs of Chicago recalled, "I couldn't buy maybe once a week a couple of pounds of meat. . . . The rest of the days, we had to live on half a pound of baloney." Chicago teachers used their own money to buy lunches for their students. Thousands of families at the time couldn't afford to feed themselves.

In 1933, President Franklin Roosevelt began what was called the New Deal. He called for the U.S. government to help the poor across the country. Illinois, with more than 7 million people, was one of the largest states, and it received a large share of this aid. This money did not end the Great Depression, but it softened the blow for Illinoisans and other Americans. The state government also gave aid to people out of work, homeless, and desperate for food.

WORD TO KNOW

nuclear weapon *a bomb that uses the huge amount of power stored inside the atoms of some materials to create large explosions*

MINI-BIO

MANUEL PEREZ JR.: WAR HERO

Of the many Illinoisans who served in World War II, Manuel Perez Jr. (1923–1945) was one of the bravest. In 1945, on the island of Luzon, Perez was a lead scout. He single-handedly secured an enemy position that had blocked the advance of his company. Although later killed in action, his heroics inspired the other soldiers in his unit. After his death, Perez was awarded the Congressional Medal of Honor, the highest honor the United States gives to members of the military. The city of Chicago honored Perez by naming a plaza (at 26th and Kolin) and an elementary school after him.

WORLD WAR II

What ended the hard times across the United States? It was the coming of World War II in 1939. Most Americans didn't want to fight in a second European war. In the Midwest, the *Chicago Tribune* led the call to keep the United States out of European affairs. But Roosevelt wanted to help Great Britain and its allies fight Germany, and sent them aid. He also began strengthening the U.S. military, in case the United States was drawn into the war. On December 7, 1941, Japan launched a surprise attack on the U.S. naval base in Pearl Harbor, Hawaii. Suddenly, the need for weapons and supplies increased.

Soon the United States was fighting both Japan and Germany. Illinois sent 972,000 residents into the military, and 22,192 of them gave their lives defending their country.

During the war, building weapons provided factory jobs for millions of Americans. In Illinois, a Chicago auto plant produced bomber planes, while other factories in the state made boats, aircraft parts, and vehicles for moving large guns. At Rock Island and other towns, Illinoisans made ammunition, producing more of it than any other factories in other states. And scientists in Chicago played a part in developing the first **nuclear weapon**.

During World War II, factories needed workers. This helped African Americans get jobs. But many still faced tough living conditions. In

Chicago, housing was in short supply. Five or six people might share a one-room apartment. American women also went to work in the factories. In Illinois, the number of working women rose by more than 50 percent. During these years, newly arrived workers from Mexico helped support the war effort by working in Illinois factories.

POSTWAR PROGRESS

When the war ended in 1945, the United States entered another period of explosive economic growth. Illinois shared in this wealth. People in the southern part of the state went north, looking for work in Chicago and other industrial cities. Some African Americans continued to move to Illinois from the South, looking for work.

Illinois workers at the Ford assembly line in the Highland Park factory

Major electrical manufacturers made radios, TVs, and other products. They also made electrical equipment for the military.

Through the 1950s and 1960s, more city residents, especially in Chicago, moved out into the suburbs. Farmland was turned into housing developments. And workers either drove or took the train to their jobs in the city. New highways made it easier for people to commute, though long traffic tie-ups became common. The problem only grew worse over the years, so that by the early 2000s, Chicago roads were among the most jammed in the country.

Most of the residents who moved from the cities to the suburbs were white. Meanwhile, the African American population in cities rose. Chicago, for example, had just under 500,000 blacks in 1950, and just over 800,000 ten years later. African Americans often faced crowded living conditions in run-down slum sections of cities. They also faced prejudice.

The 1950s and 1960s saw the rise of the civil rights movement in the South. The movement stirred people of color in Chicago and the rest of

Civil rights activist Jesse Jackson was the head of Operation Breadbasket in Chicago during the 1960s. This was a program sponsored by the Southern Christian Leadership Conference.

Illinois to fight for their rights and demand equality. Jesse Jackson made Chicago his base to become a national civil rights leader and a **candidate** for president.

During the 1960s, the Vietnam War also sparked protests across the country. One of the most famous came in 1968 in Chicago during the Democratic National Convention. Outside the hall where the Democrats met, Chicago police fought antiwar protesters. The city was criticized for dealing brutally with the protesters.

ILLINOIS TODAY

Since the 1960s and 1970s, Illinois has seen many changes, especially in the workplace. Manufacturing has shrunk, as companies have either slashed jobs or moved them to factories in the South or overseas. Meatpacking jobs had left the state even earlier. In northern Illinois, workers have wrestled with long drives to reach city jobs. The cost of housing has soared, forcing people to move farther away from the cities to find homes they can afford. At the same time, the growth of suburbs has led to the end of the simple, quiet life people enjoyed in small farm towns.

People from around the world still choose to make Illinois their home. Large numbers of Spanish-speaking immigrants from Mexico and Central America continue to settle in the state. In some cities, Mexican Americans have gained political strength because of

MINI-BIO

RICHARD J. DALEY: CHICAGO MAYOR

Illinoisans knew him as "Boss" or "Duh Mare." From 1955 until 1976, Mayor Richard J. Daley (1902–1976) ran the city of Chicago. He helped bring new highways and buildings to the city, but his foes complained about his tactics. They said he ruled liked an emperor, not an elected official who was supposed to listen to voters. Daley became one of the most famous mayors in U.S. history, and his son Richard M. Daley followed in his footsteps, becoming mayor of Chicago in 1989.

? Want to know more?
See http://www.chicagohistory.info/stories/daley/

WORDS TO KNOW

candidate *a person who runs for a political office*

Mexican Americans celebrate Cinco de Mayo in Chicago. Latinos are just one group of immigrants who have a strong presence in Illinois.

MINI-BIO

HAROLD WASHINGTON: POLITICAL LEADER

One of the first black political heroes was Harold Washington (1922–1987). Trained as a lawyer, he served as an Illinois law-maker for 14 years. In 1977, he ran for mayor of Chicago, but lost. Six years later, he ran again and won, becoming Chicago's first black mayor. His appeal to other African Americans led to his victory. Under him, blacks were given important government jobs in the city. Washington died just after winning a second term as mayor in 1987.

their increasing numbers. Immigrants from Africa, Eastern Europe, and Asia have come to Illinois as well. The new arrivals and their children bring new energy and ideas to the state.

Illinois today is a land of economic extremes. Teens in wealthy Chicago suburbs go to some of the best schools in the country. At the opposite end of the spectrum are some economically disad-vantaged areas where schools struggle to meet the needs of their students.

Running a state costs lots of money. Highways have to be main-tained, public schools need books and good buildings, and government workers have to be paid. Sometimes keeping up with all the expenses is difficult. Illinois has tried to find ways to raise money, without increasing taxes on families and business. The state government's debt in 2006 was almost $18 billion and rising. Some state and city funds were being used to prepare for possible terrorist attacks. Illinois had several likely targets, such as the Sears Tower and the transportation system. But whatever the state's challenges, Illinoisans believe they can meet them.

THINK ABOUT IT!

Security at Any Cost

PRO

One way to fight terrorism and keep people safe is to have security cameras in more places. So the city of Chicago added more cameras to its streets. Some people believe that cameras are a good way to keep an eye on everyone. For instance, Mayor Richard M. Daley has called the surveillance cameras "the next best thing to having police officers stationed at every potential trouble spot."

CON

Some people are concerned that civil rights are being compromised when everyone is watched so much. And they worry that soon cameras will be everywhere. As Ed Yohnka of the American Civil Liberties Union explains, "You put the cameras up today, then you start adding facial recognition technology, then you start recording it, then you don't just use them in high-crime areas."

Sources: *The Chicago Tribune,* December 3, 2006; *The Christian Science Monitor,* July 30, 2003

READ
ABOUT

Illinois thrives on
the productivity
of its hardworking
people.

CHAPTER SIX

PEOPLE

★

A NEWLY ARRIVED FAMILY FROM INDIA PRAYS IN A HINDU TEMPLE IN LEMONT. Guatemalans bustle about in their Chicago restaurant, serving food to eager diners. African American students share ideas for their next class at Carbondale's Southern Illinois University. A Hispanic couple renovates a house as they await the birth of their first child. A farmer, whose roots in Illinois go back more than 100 years, drives a tractor across his fields. These are just some of the different people who call Illinois home.

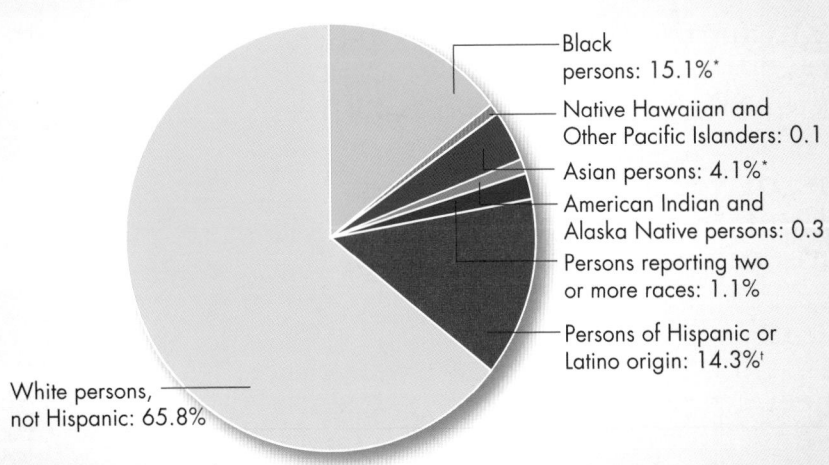

Getting ready for a parade in Beardstown, Illinois. Illinois is home to cultures from all over the world.

People QuickFacts

Black persons: 15.1%*

Native Hawaiian and Other Pacific Islanders: 0.1

Asian persons: 4.1%*

American Indian and Alaska Native persons: 0.3

Persons reporting two or more races: 1.1%

Persons of Hispanic or Latino origin: 14.3%†

White persons, not Hispanic: 65.8%

*Includes persons reporting only one race
†Hispanics may be of any race, so also are included in applicable race categories
Source: U.S. Census Bureau, 2005

AT HOME IN ILLINOIS

Chicago and its surrounding counties make up about 75 percent of the state's population. Small cities, rural towns, farmland, and forests are found throughout the central and southern parts of the state. And some entire counties in those regions have fewer people than some of Chicago's larger neighborhoods.

PEOPLE FROM DIFFERENT LANDS

The United States is a nation of immigrants, and that's true for Illinois, too. The state's residents trace their roots to more than 100 countries. The largest groups are German, Irish, African American, Mexican, and Polish. Chicago has the second-largest Mexican American population in the country, second only to Los Angeles. It also has the second-largest Polish population in the world, after Warsaw, Poland. Some of the other countries represented in the state are Nigeria, Ethiopia, Ghana, Egypt, India, Pakistan, Serbia, Ukraine, Cambodia, and Brazil. The greatest mix of ethnic groups is in Chicago and the surrounding counties.

Illinoisans speak dozens of languages in their homes, with many using both English and the language of their native land. There are 9.5 million residents over the age of 18. Of these, 7.7 million say they use only English at home. Spanish is the second-most spoken language. This reflects the large growth in the Latino population—some 69 percent between 1990 and 2000. Immigrants from Mexico, Puerto Rico, and the rest of Latin America make Latinos the fastest-growing ethnic group in the state.

Where Illinoisans Live

The colors on this map indicate population density throughout the state. The darker the color, the more people live there.

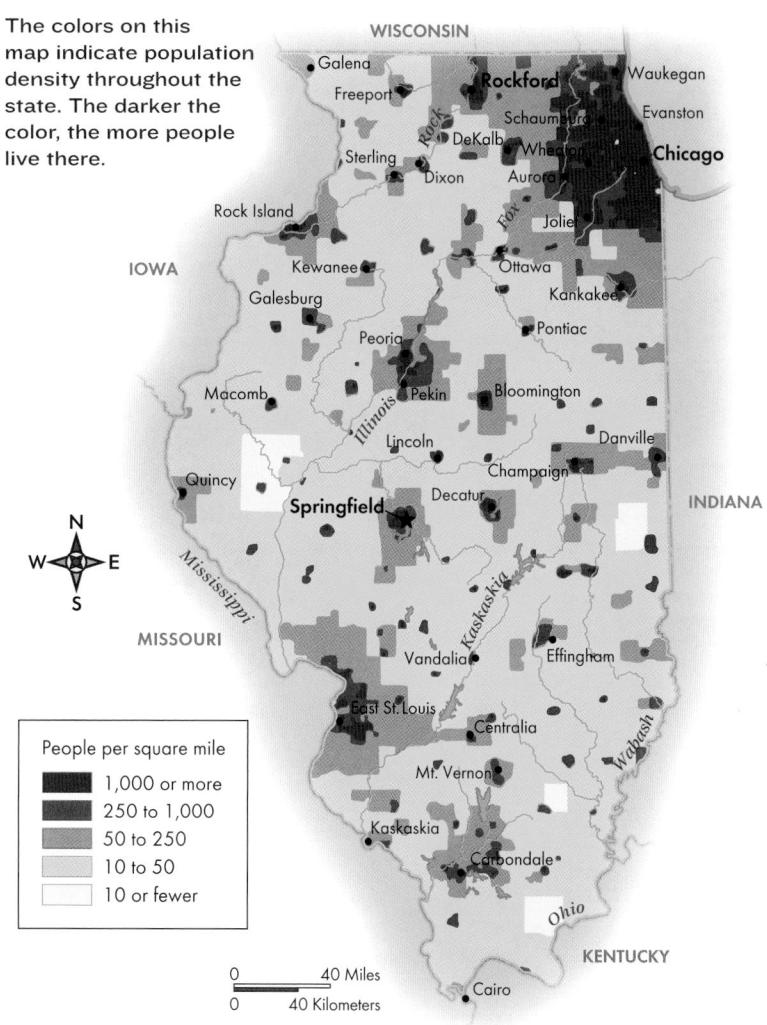

People per square mile

- 1,000 or more
- 250 to 1,000
- 50 to 250
- 10 to 50
- 10 or fewer

The 2006 estimated population of almost 12.8 million made Illinois the fifth most populated state in the Union.

70

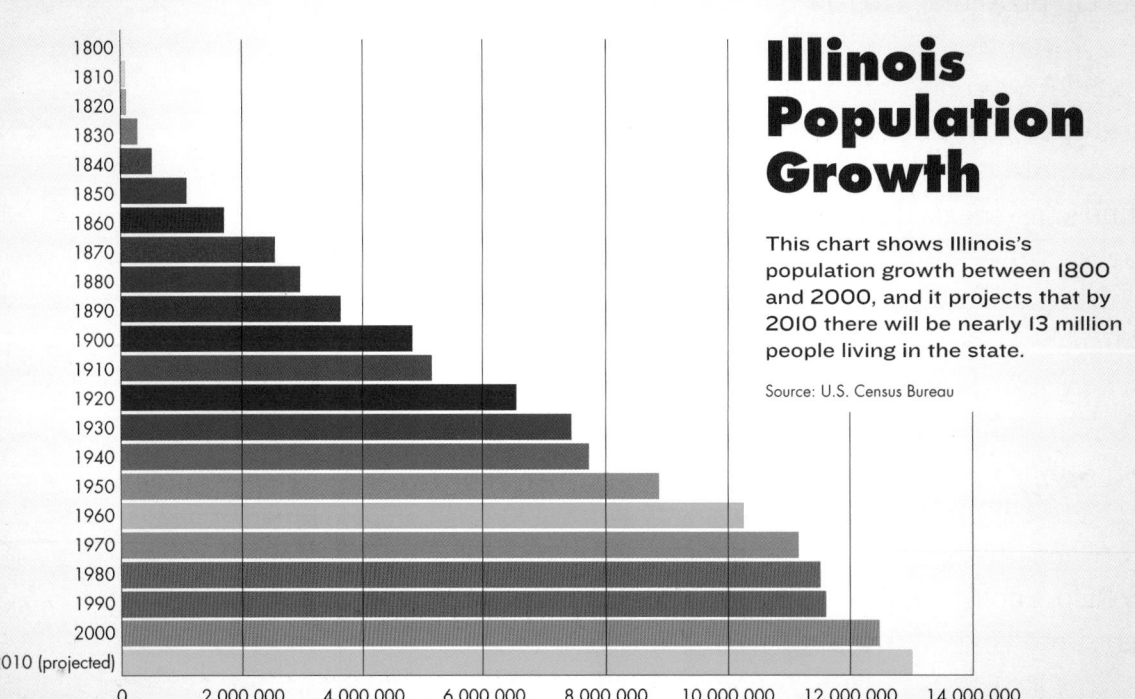

Illinois neighborhoods and schools represent a range of races, heritages, and nationalities.

Illinois Population Growth

This chart shows Illinois's population growth between 1800 and 2000, and it projects that by 2010 there will be nearly 13 million people living in the state.

Source: U.S. Census Bureau

Year	Population (bar chart)
1800	
1810	
1820	
1830	
1840	
1850	
1860	
1870	
1880	
1890	
1900	
1910	
1920	
1930	
1940	
1950	
1960	
1970	
1980	
1990	
2000	
2010 (projected)	

0 — 2,000,000 — 4,000,000 — 6,000,000 — 8,000,000 — 10,000,000 — 12,000,000 — 14,000,000

FROM THE CITY TO THE COUNTRY

City life varies for Illinoisans, depending on their income and preferences. In Chicago, people might live in high-rise condos that tower 60 or 70 stories above the city streets. Or they might live in brick two-flats, which are two-family homes, scattered throughout many neighborhoods. The city also has single-family homes. In Chicago, many residents can easily walk to shops, businesses, and recreation. The train system, called the El (for "elevated"), runs on tracks above city streets and sometimes runs underground as well. If you want to avoid the heavy traffic, the El is the way to go!

Drive just a few hours outside of Chicago or the other major cities, and life changes dramatically. Many jobs in the rural areas are tied to farming: raising crops, making equipment for farms, and turning crops into food. Life in a rural town is slower than in the city. Most people don't rush off to work at distant jobs.

Big City Life

This list shows the population of Illinois's biggest cities.

Chicago 2,833,321
Aurora 170,617
Rockford 155,138
Naperville 142,901
Joliet 142,702
Springfield 116,482

Source: U.S. Census Bureau, 2006 estimate

Volunteers in a community garden project in Beardstown

BESIDES ENGLISH, WHICH LANGUAGES ARE MOST COMMONLY SPOKEN IN ILLINOIS HOMES?

Language	Number of Speakers
Spanish	931,780
Polish	158,495
German	56,995
Tagalog (Filipino language)	56,670
Chinese	55,575
Italian	48,205
Korean	36,525
Greek	36,005
French	33,605
Russian	32,545

ILLINOIS FOOD FACTS

- In 1937, packaged boxes of Kraft macaroni and cheese were first produced in Chicago.
- Collinsville is the horseradish capital of the world, and each year it hosts a festival honoring the hot stuff.
- In 2006, Illinois announced a ban on all junk foods in elementary and middle schools.

HOW TO TALK LIKE AN ILLINOISAN

On the road, Illinoisans have some terms you might not hear anywhere else. Drivers who slow down to stare at an accident are "gapers," and the traffic tie-up they can create is a "gaper's block." And while some Americans pull over to stretch their legs and get a snack at a highway rest area, drivers in Illinois stop at an "oasis."

Soft drinks are known as "pop." And what do Chicagoans call their famous sports teams? Da Bulls and da Bears.

HOW TO EAT LIKE AN ILLINOISAN

When you think of Illinois food, you probably think of Chicago's deep-dish pizza. But don't forget all the fresh fruits and vegetables from Illinois farms. There are apples and berries, peaches and pears, beans and broccoli. Do you love fresh corn on the cob? Then, Illinois is the place for you! It is a leader in corn production. Beef is also popular in the state, and German and Polish dishes such as sausages and sauerkraut are favorites for some. See the menu on the opposite page, and dig in!

Chicago-style deep-dish pizza

MENU
WHAT'S ON THE MENU IN ILLINOIS?

Hot Dog

A boiled or steamed all-beef dog sits in a poppy-seed roll, smothered with fresh tomato, onions, a slice of dill pickle, relish, hot peppers, mustard, and celery salt. Ketchup, however, is a no-no on a true Chicago dog.

Burgoo

Throw meat and veggies in a pot, and what have you got? A hearty stew called burgoo! Settlers from Kentucky brought this tasty dish into Illinois long ago, and it's still popular in the southern part of Illinois.

Popcorn

Most folks like popcorn, but Illinois has made this healthy treat the state snack. More than 300 farms raise popping corn, making Illinois the third-largest producer of popcorn in the United States.

Deep-Dish Pizza

The Chicago deep-dish pizza first appeared during the 1940s. A thick crust is spread over a round pan with tall sides. The crust is often partially baked, then taken out of the oven so meat, cheese, and veggies can be added. Stuffed pizza, also popular around the Chicago area, has a second layer of crust over the other ingredients.

TRY THIS RECIPE
Pumpkin Seeds

Illinois leads the nation in growing pumpkins, and state cooks have found plenty of ways to make them great to eat. Deep inside the pumpkin, there's something else that tastes good and is good for you: the seeds! Here's a recipe for toasting your own pumpkin seeds. Be sure to ask an adult to help.

Ingredients:

- 2 cups pumpkin seeds
- 1 quart water
- 2 tablespoons salt
- 1 tablespoon vegetable oil

Instructions:

1. Turn on the oven to 250°F.
2. Separate the seeds from the stringy stuff around them. Remove any cut seeds.
3. Put the water and salt in a pan and bring to a boil. Add the seeds and boil for 10 minutes.
4. Drain the seeds, then spread them on a kitchen towel or paper towel and pat dry.
5. Place the seeds in a bowl; toss with the oil.
6. Spread evenly on a large cookie sheet or roasting pan.
7. Place the pan in a preheated oven and roast the seeds for 30 to 40 minutes. Stir every 10 minutes, until crisp and golden brown.
8. Cool the seeds, then shell and eat them. You can also pack them in airtight containers or zip-top bags and refrigerate until ready to eat.

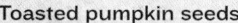

Toasted pumpkin seeds

MINI-BIO

CARL SANDBURG: PRIZEWINNING POET

Carl Sandburg (1878–1967) was one of America's best-loved poets. The son of Swedish immigrants, Sandburg was born in Galesburg and made his name in Chicago, where he wrote about common people of the Midwest. In addition to poetry, he wrote news articles and was active in politics. He won two Pulitzer Prizes, which honor outstanding U.S. writers, photographers, and musicians. One of Sandburg's most famous works was a six-volume biography of another great Illinoisan, Abraham Lincoln.

 **Want to know more?** See carl-sandburg.com/biography.htm

THE THREE R'S AND MORE

Whether they live in large cities, small towns, or somewhere in between, Illinois kids can attend a variety of schools—there are more than 6,000 of them altogether! Local governments run public schools, while some churches and other organizations run private schools. Charter schools combine money from the government with donations to meet their costs. Charter schools sometimes focus on a particular type of study, such as math and science or technical skills. Most are in or near the state's largest cities.

Illinois also offers students and scholars from around the globe a variety of colleges and universities. The University of Illinois has its main campus in Champaign and the neighboring town of Urbana. Additional branches are in Springfield and Chicago. Other state schools include Southern Illinois University in Carbondale, Northern Illinois University in DeKalb, Illinois State University in Normal, Eastern Illinois University in Charleston, and Western Illinois University in Macomb. The state's top private universities are Bradley University in Peoria, the University of Chicago, and Northwestern, located just north of Chicago in Evanston.

TALENTED WRITERS

People around the world have turned to literature created by talented Illinoisans. L. Frank Baum was a Chicago resident when he created Dorothy, the Scarecrow, and the other famous characters in *The Wonderful Wizard of Oz*. Baum wrote 13 more books set in the land of Oz, as well as a host of others. Edgar Rice Burroughs, the creator of Tarzan, was born in Chicago. And Ernest Hemingway was born in the neighboring town of Oak Park. Hemingway wrote some of the most popular novels of the 20th century, including *A Farewell to Arms* and *The Sun Also Rises*. Science-fiction writer Ray Bradbury came from Waukegan. He set his book *Dandelion Wine* in a fictional town modeled on his hometown.

One popular children's writer is Blue Balliett, a Chicago teacher. She sets her work at some of the city's famous sites. Another Illinois writer is Richard Peck. He was born in Decatur and loves writing for young readers. Some of his books are *A Long Way from Chicago, Monster Night at Grandma's House*, and *Are You in the House Alone?*

MINI-BIO

SANDRA CISNEROS: CHICAGO WRITER

As a child, Sandra Cisneros (1954–) grew up speaking Spanish in a Mexican American home in Chicago. Writing in English, she has become one of the most famous Latina writers in the world. She drew on her experiences in Chicago for her best-loved work, *The House on Mango Street*. Cisneros has also written poetry and essays. Her work often features strong women trying to show they deserve the same rights and respect as men.

? Want to know more? See sandracisneros.com

ARCHITECTS TO ACTORS

One of the most famous architects in the world was Frank Lloyd Wright. He worked in Oak Park for many years. And two of his well-known buildings are Chicago's Frederick C. Robie House and the Avery and Queen Coonley House. Artist George Peter Alexander Healy was born in Boston but lived in Chicago for a time. He is best remembered for his portraits, including those of Daniel Webster, John C. Calhoun, and presidents such as John Quincy Adams, Ulysses S. Grant, and Andrew Jackson.

Today, Illinois—and Chicago in particular—is the setting for many popular films. The state has also produced a number of filmmakers and stars. Harold Ramis, the director of comedies such as *Caddyshack* and *Groundhog Day*, was born in Chicago. He had a fea-

Frank Lloyd Wright poses in front of his 1909 prairie-style Robie House, located near the University of Chicago campus.

Ferris Bueller's Day Off, starring Matthew Broderick, was directed by Chicago native Harold Ramis and shot mostly in Illinois.

tured role in the film *Ghostbusters*, which starred another Illinois native, Bill Murray. A more recent film star who was raised in the Chicago area is Vince Vaughn. Chicago is also known as a major theater center, with nationally known professional stages and schools for training actors, directors, and writers.

MUSIC WORLD

Some big-name musicians have hailed from Illinois. The great jazz trumpeter Miles Davis was born in Alton and moved to East St. Louis. Jazz and popular music

MINI-BIO

BILL MURRAY: FUNNY MAN

Bill Murray (1950—) was born in Wilmette and learned the ins and outs of comedy performing live onstage at Chicago's Second City, one of the most famous comedy clubs in the nation. From there he went on to TV's *Saturday Night Live* before making the jump to films. He appeared in such classic comedies as *Caddyshack*, *Stripes*, *Ghostbusters*, and *Groundhog Day*—which was filmed in Woodstock, Illinois. Murray has won praise for playing serious roles, too.

composer Quincy Jones comes from Chicago, which has been a center for the blues for decades. Musicians such as Buddy Guy and Muddy Waters often recorded at Chess Records, a famous blues recording studio. Hip-hop artist Kanye West hails from Chicago. In 2006, he won three Grammy Awards, which are given each year to the best musicians and songwriters from around the world.

While playing for the Chicago Bulls, Jordan led the NBA in scoring nine times.

MINI-BIO

MICHAEL JORDAN: HIS AIRNESS

Is he the greatest basketball player ever? Lots of people say yes. Michael Jordan (1963–) was born in Brooklyn, New York, grew up in North Carolina, and played college basketball for the University of North Carolina Tar Heels. But he reached super-star status as a guard for the Chicago Bulls. He led the team to an NBA championship in 1991 and followed that with two more titles in 1992 and 1993—a "three-peat." He then retired from the game but couldn't stay away. He returned to the Bulls and led the team to another "three-peat" in the years 1996–1998. Over the years, he was named MVP numerous times, and he played on the 1984 and 1992 gold medal–winning Olympic teams. His famous slam dunks earned him the nicknames "His Airness" and "Air Jordan."

PLAYING BALL

Illinois is home to some great professional sports teams—and to some of the most die-hard sports fans anywhere! In the 1920s, Red Grange, the "Galloping Ghost," attended the University of Illinois and played for the Chicago Bears. More than 80 years later, those Bears battled in the 2007 Super Bowl, but lost to the Indianapolis Colts.

On the basketball court, the Chicago Bulls have been wowing fans for decades. One standout is Michael Jordan—"MJ" to his fans. He led the Bulls to six NBA championships.

Illinois loves baseball, too. The Chicago Cubs and Chicago White Sox are fan favorites. And the White Sox captured the World Series in 2005.

Acclaimed musician and producer Quincy Jones was born in Chicago. He has received more than 25 Grammy Awards.

The state boasts athletes and artists, teachers and farmers, chefs and scholars. It's no wonder that people from all different backgrounds and interests make Illinois their home.

MINI-BIO

DICK BUTKUS: FOOTBALL LEGEND

Sports Illustrated called him "the most feared man in the game" in 1970. Dick Butkus (1942–) was born in Chicago and played college football for the University of Illinois. Then he was drafted by his hometown Chicago Bears. He was known for being one of the toughest tacklers on the field. He regularly led his team in tackles, interceptions, forced fumbles, and fumble recoveries. In 1973, he had to retire from the game because of a knee injury. He was named to the NFL's all-decade team in the 1960s and 1970s, and he was inducted into the Pro Football Hall of Fame in 1979. In the years since, Butkus has been a TV commentator and sports broadcaster.

READ ABOUT

Inside the house chamber in the state capitol. The house is where representatives debate and pass laws.

CHAPTER SEVEN

GOVERNMENT

★

HAVE YOU EVER WONDERED HOW COURTS AND TRIALS REALLY WORK? Teenagers in Illinois sometimes find out firsthand. They can act as lawyers and serve on special juries. They talk to judges and hear cases to decide on punishment after a teen has admitted guilt. All this happens in a program known as teen courts. These special courts play an important part in the legal system. The Illinois Youth Court Association created the first one in 1996 in Round Lake Beach. Now the state has more than 100 such courts. Read more about this later in the chapter. Now let's learn about how the state government is run.

SEE IT HERE!

OLD BUT NOT FORGOTTEN

After work began on the current state capitol in 1868, the Old State Capitol was used as the courthouse for Sangamon County. The state bought the old building in 1961 and began to restore it. Each outer stone in the walls was taken down and numbered, then put back in place after work on the inside was done. The Old State Capitol reopened in 1968 and is now a state historic site. Abraham Lincoln worked in the building, arguing law cases, and gave his famous "House Divided" speech there. In 1865, his body was taken there before his burial in Springfield.

WHERE IT ALL HAPPENS

Over the years, Illinois has had three capital cities: Kaskaskia (1818–1820), Vandalia (1820–1839), and Springfield (1839–present). Today, the heart of Illinois's government is in Springfield's state capitol, a domed building that is 74 feet (22.5 m) taller than the U.S. Capitol in Washington, D.C. The Illinois building—sometimes called the State House—has four floors, and visitors can watch lawmakers at work from a balcony. The governor also keeps an office in the state capitol.

Capital City

This map shows places of interest in Springfield, Illinois's capital city.

Capitol Facts

Here are some fascinating facts about Illinois's state capitol.

Exterior height	405 feet (123 m)
Number of stories high	4
Length	379 feet (116 m)
Width	268 feet (82 m)
Surrounding park	9 acres (3.6 ha)
Location	2nd Street and Monroe
Construction dates	1868–1888
Cost of construction	$4.5 million

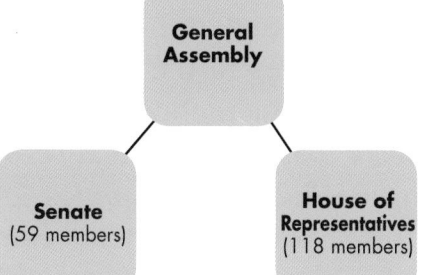

The Capitol in Springfield is located at 2nd and Monroe streets. A bronze statue of Abraham Lincoln stands out front.

Illinois State Government

EXECUTIVE BRANCH
Carries out state laws

| Secretary of State | Treasurer | Governor | Attorney General | Comptroller | Lieutenant Governor |

LEGISLATIVE BRANCH
Makes and passes state laws

General Assembly

Senate (59 members)

House of Representatives (118 members)

JUDICIAL BRANCH
Enforces state laws

State Supreme Court

Appellate Court (5 districts)

Circuit Courts (22)

The governor also does business and sees guests in the Executive Mansion, a short stroll from the state capitol. In 2003, Governor Rod Blagojevich broke tradition when he chose to live in Chicago rather than at the Executive Mansion. Much of the home, however, remained open to the public for tours.

The Illinois Supreme Court has its own building in Springfield. The building opened in 1908 and includes a law library as well as offices and a courtroom. Unlike Supreme Court justices in some states, those in Illinois do not have to move to the state capital when they are elected to office.

The state government, like the federal government, has three separate branches. The legislative branch makes laws, the executive branch carries out the laws (and often proposes new ones), and the judicial branch makes sure the laws are enforced fairly.

THE LEGISLATIVE BRANCH

Illinois's lawmakers form the General Assembly, which includes the House of Representatives and the Senate. House members usually represent one or two towns or one part of a city, while senators represent voters in a larger geographic area. Members of either body can **sponsor** a bill, which is the blueprint for a new law. The bill is first sent to one or more committees, where it is accepted, changed, or rejected. If the bill is not rejected, it moves to the full house or senate—depending on whether the sponsor was a representative or a senator. If the full body votes for the bill, it moves to the other part of

WORD TO KNOW

sponsor *to act as a person who proposes or creates a bill*

Representing Illinois

This list shows the number of elected officials who represent Illinois, both on the state and national levels.

OFFICE	NUMBER	LENGTH OF TERM
State representatives	118	2 years
State senators	59	4 years
U.S. representatives	19	2 years
U.S. senators	2	6 years
Presidential electors	21	—

The Illinois governor addresses a joint session of the state house and senate. These two government bodies make up the state legislature and are responsible for creating laws.

the General Assembly for debate. In some cases, members from the two houses meet in a committee to iron out their differences over a bill.

Besides making laws for the state, Illinois lawmakers can propose changes to the state constitution, which outlines the basic structure of the government. And if members of the executive or judicial branch break the law, the legislature can remove them through a process called impeachment.

MINI-BIO

BARACK OBAMA: RISING STAR

Born in Hawaii, Barack Obama (1961–) spent part of his childhood in Indonesia. He is the son of a white American mother and a Kenyan father who had once made his living herding goats in his native land.

A Democrat, Obama first entered politics in 1996, representing a section of Chicago in the state legislature. In 2004, he became a national figure when he gave a powerful speech at the Democratic National Convention and won a seat in the U.S. Senate. In 2007, he announced his candidacy for the presidential election of 2008.

NINIAN EDWARDS: TERRITORIAL GOVERNOR

Even before it became a state, Illinois had a governor, and he emerged as one of Illinois's most successful politicians. Ninian Edwards (1775–1833) came to Illinois from Kentucky in 1809 to serve as the first and only governor of the Illinois Territory. A wealthy man, Edwards stuck out from the simple frontier settlers he governed. He wore fancy clothes, had a huge farm, and raised racehorses. Still, he won the respect of the voters, who elected him one of Illinois's first two U.S. senators after it became a state in 1818. In 1826, Edwards was chosen governor of the state.

THE EXECUTIVE BRANCH

The executive branch in Illinois has six positions elected by the voters. The governor is the leader of the executive branch and chooses people to lead various executive departments. The General Assembly, however, must approve these choices. The governor also proposes an annual budget, but the assembly has the final say on how much money is spent and where it goes.

The lieutenant governor of Illinois steps in to lead the executive branch if the governor is out of state or otherwise not able to govern. Day to day, the lieutenant governor leads several committees. These might focus on such issues as the condition of rural towns or the health of the Illinois River.

The secretary of state oversees more departments than any other member of Illinois's executive branch. Voting, driving privileges, the state library—the secretary of state keeps tabs on all these and more. No other secretary of state in the United States has as many duties as the one who serves in Illinois.

The attorney general is the state's top lawyer. In that role, the attorney general tries to protect residents against scams, defends the interests of the state and towns in court, and helps victims of violent crime.

When it comes to numbers, the comptroller makes sure they always add up. You could call the comptroller the state's accountant. One duty of the office is to pay the state's bills.

This is the Macoupin County courthouse in Carlinville. Each county in the state has its own local government and court system.

The treasurer is another important numbers person in the executive branch. Acting as the state's banker, the treasurer invests the state's money, searching for safe ways to make more of it. The treasurer can also invest the money in companies that create more jobs for state workers.

THE JUDICIAL BRANCH

The judicial branch in Illinois has several layers. At the bottom are the circuit courts. When people are accused of breaking the law, they are brought to circuit courts to defend themselves. If criminals are found guilty, the circuit court judges determine their sentence. Most judges are elected. Circuit judges elect a chief judge for each of the 22 circuits. The circuit judges also choose judges called associates, who can hear most cases.

WEIRD AND WACKY LAWS

Most Illinois laws make sense, by protecting people or improving their lives. But some state and local laws might seem downright strange. Here are a few weird laws found in Illinois.

- People in Joliet can be fined for not saying the town's name right—it's JOE-liet, not JOLLY-et.
- It's illegal to fly a kite in Chicago—but people still do!
- Don't hum while strolling the streets in Cicero on a Sunday—it's against the law.
- Something's weird in Normal—you can't make a face at dogs there.

ILLINOIS PRESIDENTS

Abraham Lincoln (1809–1865) was the 16th president of the United States and served from 1861 to 1865. Born in Kentucky, Lincoln and his parents settled in Illinois in 1830. He became a successful Springfield lawyer and a politician. As president, he led the United States through the Civil War.

Ulysses S. Grant (1822–1885) was the 18th president of the United States and served from 1869 to 1877. Before becoming a general in the Union army, he spent a brief time in Galena. He kept a home there through his presidency. His heroics during the Civil War led to his election as president.

Ronald Wilson Reagan (1911–2004) was the 40th president of the United States and served from 1981 to 1989. Reagan was born in Tampico, went to high school in nearby Dixon, and attended Eureka College. After school, he headed to California, where he later became a movie star and a politician.

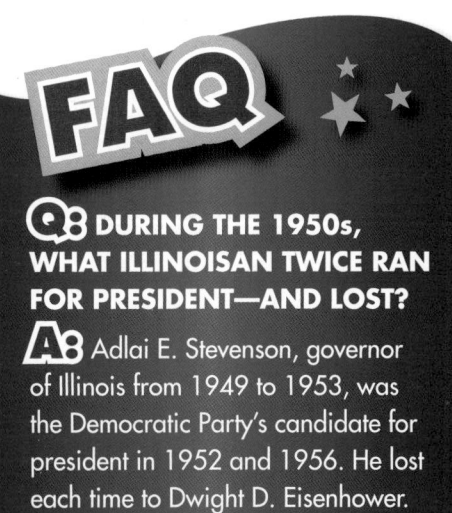

Q: DURING THE 1950s, WHAT ILLINOISAN TWICE RAN FOR PRESIDENT—AND LOST?

A: Adlai E. Stevenson, governor of Illinois from 1949 to 1953, was the Democratic Party's candidate for president in 1952 and 1956. He lost each time to Dwight D. Eisenhower.

Someone found guilty can challenge the decision in the state's appellate courts. These courts also hear the appeals of decisions made by government agencies. The last place to appeal a decision is in the Illinois Supreme Court. Its seven members hear cases that challenge state laws to see if they violate the constitution.

GOVERNMENT CLOSER TO HOME

Like the other states, Illinois has lawmakers and executives who govern on the local level. Counties have their own government. Within the counties are different kinds of political units called municipalities: cities, towns, and villages. In both the counties and the municipalities, voters elect people to serve on boards that pass local ordinances and collect taxes. Some counties have townships, where voters gather at annual meetings to decide how to spend tax money and address property issues. All the forms of local government provide for schools, law enforcement, libraries, fire protection, and other essential public services. The Illinois Constitution and the General Assembly set some limits on what local governments can do, such as what kind of taxes they can charge and how high they can be.

Illinois also has governing bodies called special districts. The district usually does just one thing, such as taking care of parks, providing water or sewer services,

or ensuring public health. Illinois has almost 7,000 local district governments—more than any other state. At the local district level, various public officials carry out the executive duties. County boards are headed by a president, while large cities usually have mayors. Some towns hire a professional town manager to carry out the policies their elected boards approve.

Illinois is truly a democratic state, known for giving its citizens an opportunity to have a voice in local politics through council and town meetings and boards.

WORD TO KNOW

peers *people of a similar age or background*

TEEN COURTS

At the beginning of this chapter, you read about teen courts. Here is how the program works. Youths who commit crimes such as destroying property, starting a fight, or drinking alcohol can choose to appear in court before their **peers**. The offenders must be between 13 and 16 years old and have never broken the law before. The teens must first admit they are guilty. Then they explain the details of their case to the teen jurors. The jurors are volunteers with an interest in law—and in

Illinois Counties

This map shows the 102 counties in Illinois. Springfield, the state capital, is indicated with a star.

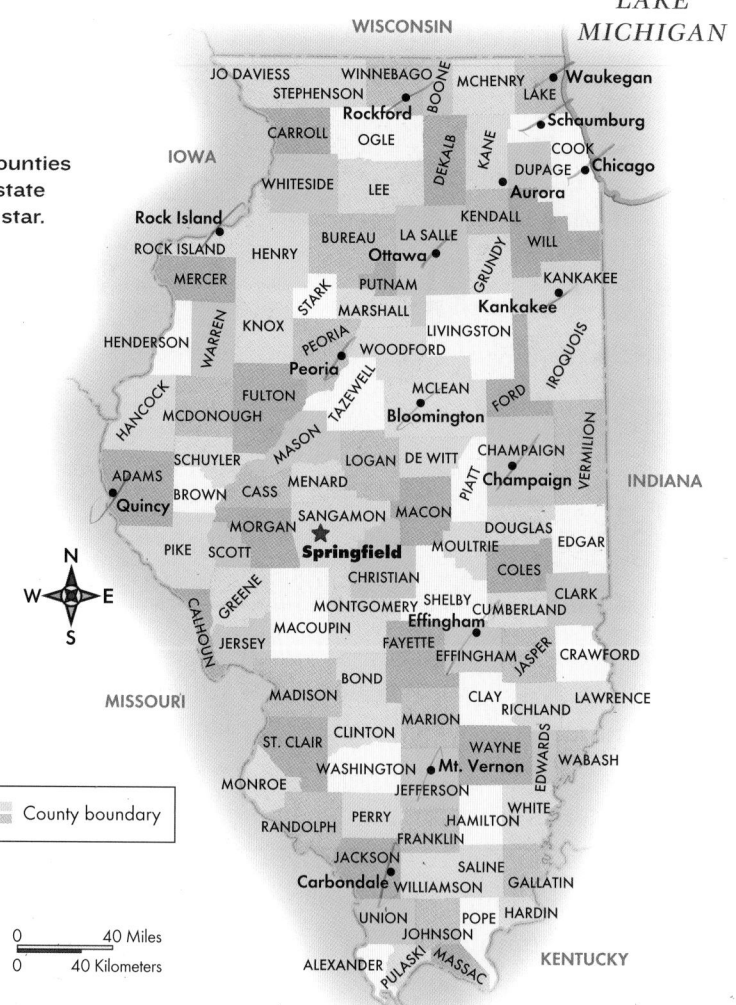

County boundary

helping friends, neighbors, and classmates learn from their mistakes. The "trials" are usually held during lunchtime or after school. After hearing the case, the jurors deliver a sentence. Perhaps the offenders will have to do community service or take a class to change their behavior. If the offenders don't do their service, school officials step in.

Do the teen courts work? Studies say yes. Kids sent to teen courts are less likely to break the law in the future. Julie Pawl set up Illinois's first teen court. She says that for many of the teens, "It is their first experience with realizing that the decisions they make really can affect the rest of their lives." And the young jurors get a better understanding of the legal system, which just might spark their interest in becoming a judge or lawmaker someday.

Teen offenders may have to participate in community service as part of their court decision. Here a group of teens in Chicago clean up graffiti as part of their community service to the city.

State Flag

Illinois's flag was adopted in 1915, after a campaign by the Daughters of the American Revolution. Originally, it displayed the state seal on a white field. Initially, a prize of $25 dollars was offered for the best design for the state flag. Thirty-five designs were submitted, and the design that was ultimately chosen was by Lucy Derwent of Rockford.

In 1969, Chief Petty Officer Bruce McDaniel of Waverly was serving in Vietnam when he noticed, unlike the other state flags hanging in his mess hall, the Illinois flag didn't display its state's name. McDaniel began an effort that led to the addition of the word *Illinois* to the flag on July 1, 1970.

State Seal

In 1818, when Illinois was admitted to the Union, the first General Assembly of Illinois designed a new state symbol that included the famous United States eagle with shield, resting on an olive branch and arrows, looking upward toward the constellations.

In 1825, the seal design was altered a bit: The eagle that adorned the seal had its wings pointed skyward, the constellations were removed, and the number symbol was taken out. The current seal of Illinois dates back to 1868 and resembles the original for the most part: an American eagle on a prairie, with the sun rising on the horizon. The state motto, "State Sovereignty, National Union" is also illustrated.

READ ABOUT

The Board of Trade in Chicago contributes to the overall success of the city and state economies.

CHAPTER EIGHT

ECONOMY

★

DO YOU USE A CELL PHONE TO SNAP PICTURES, WATCH VIDEO CLIPS, OR JUST CALL A FRIEND? There's a good chance it was designed in Illinois. Building systems to keep people in touch is just one of the high-tech activities that keep the Illinois economy humming. The state remains a leading agricultural producer, a source of coal, and a center for Midwest trade and business. Illinois is also a leader in medical research and a growing presence in the world of biotechnology, which uses science to improve crops, create new medicines, and find new fuels.

RICHES FROM THE EARTH

The prairie land that drew settlers in the 19th century still produces a variety of crops, from apples to zucchini. Farmland covers almost 80 percent of the state's land area. When most people think of Illinois farms, two crops come to mind: corn and soybeans. Among all the states, Illinois is second only to neighboring Iowa in raising corn, growing about 1.8 billion bushels in 2006. The state is also second in growing soybeans, producing about 482 million bushels that same year. Illinois farmers also raise hundreds of thousands of hogs, putting them among the national leaders.

Illinois farms produce a variety of crops, including corn.

Major Agricultural and Mining Products

This map shows where Illinois's major agricultural and mining products come from. See a chicken? That means poultry is raised there.

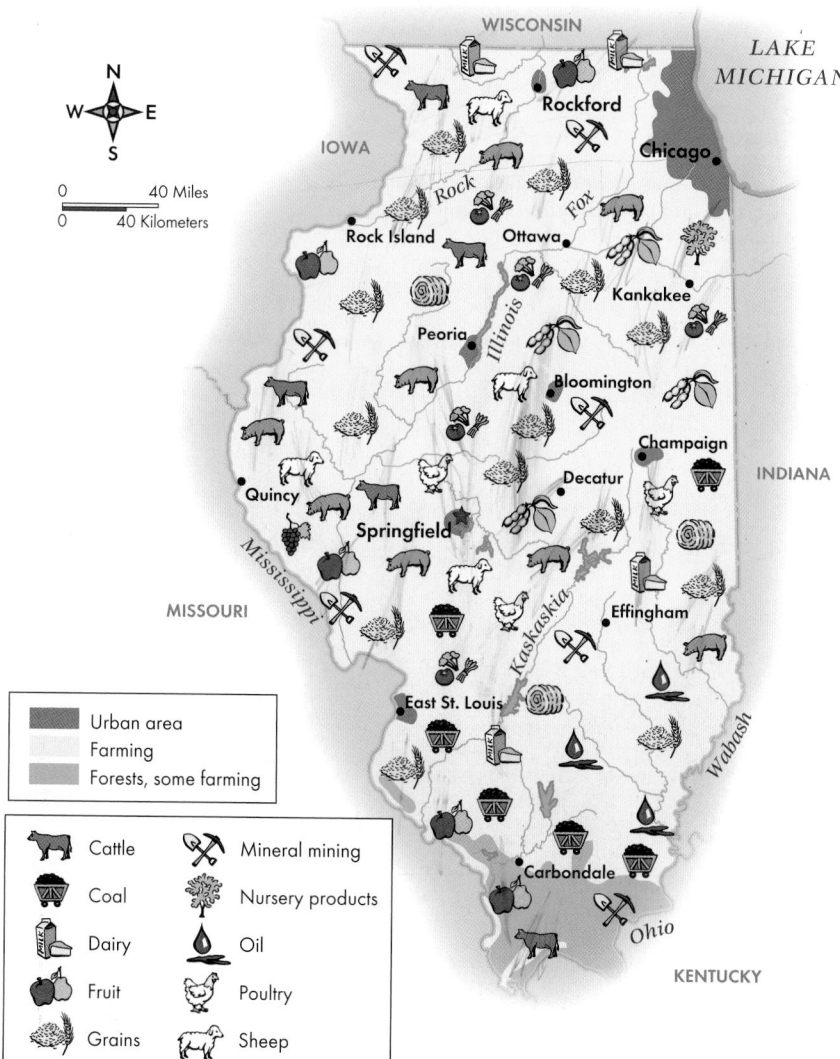

Legend:

Urban area	
Farming	
Forests, some farming	

Cattle		Mineral mining	
Coal		Nursery products	
Dairy		Oil	
Fruit		Poultry	
Grains		Sheep	
Grapes		Soybeans	
Hay		Vegetables	
Hogs			

Map labels: WISCONSIN, IOWA, Rockford, Chicago, LAKE MICHIGAN, Rock Island, Rock, Ottawa, Fox, Kankakee, Peoria, Illinois, Bloomington, Champaign, INDIANA, Quincy, Decatur, Springfield, MISSOURI, Mississippi, Kaskaskia, Effingham, East St. Louis, Carbondale, Ohio, Wabash, KENTUCKY

Scale: 0 — 40 Miles / 0 — 40 Kilometers

Compass: N, W, E, S

TOP PRODUCTS

Crops
Corn, soybeans, wheat, sorghum, hay

Livestock
Hogs, chicken, cattle, sheep

Manufacturing
Food products, machinery, electric and electronic equipment, metals, chemical products, printing and publishing

Mining
Coal, crushed stone, cement, sand and gravel

WOW

Illinois leads the nation in pumpkin production, with 12,700 acres (5,140 ha) of farmland devoted to the fall treat. The state's patches produced more than 491 million pounds (222 million kg) of pumpkins in 2006.

HOW ILLINOIS USES BIODIESEL

Like ethanol, biodiesel is a fuel produced from a common Illinois crop. Soybeans are turned into a fuel that can be used in any vehicle that runs on diesel fuel. Cars running on this soy-based fuel produce less pollution, give Illinois farmers another market for their soy crop, and help cut U.S. reliance on foreign oil. Rapeseed and soybean oils are most commonly used to make biodiesel, though other crops such as mustard, palm oil, hemp, jatropha, and even algae show promise. Animal fats can also be turned into biodiesel fuel.

Turning crops and livestock into food is also a big business in Illinois. Food processing is the state's top manufacturing activity, worth more than $13 billion each year. About $3 billion worth of the state's food products are sold overseas. The produce from Illinois's farms doesn't just end up on tables. Crops and animal products turn up in a variety of other goods, from

A farmer walks past corn storage silos. Corn is one crop that can be used to make ethanol.

ink and paper to soap and biodiesel. Archer Daniels Midland, one of the largest companies in Illinois, is a world leader in processing corn, soybeans, and other crops. Food makers Kraft and Sara Lee are also head-quartered in the state. J. L. Kraft started his cheese-making business in Chicago in 1903 by selling cheese out of a horse-drawn wagon.

Illinois farmers often use science to produce more crops. **Genetic engineering** can lead to plants that can grow with less water and fight off insects. But some people worry about changing the genetic makeup of plants and the effects it can have.

The earth in Illinois also holds one of the state's most valuable resources—coal. The Illinois Basin holds one of the largest coal supplies in the country. Most of this coal-bearing region is in Illinois, with some of it extending into Indiana and Kentucky. Illinois coal, however, creates lots of air pollution when it is burned for fuel. With concern about pollution high, demand for Illinois coal has fallen.

But various industry officials and engineers are exploring what they hope will be cleaner coal produc-tion plants. The plants would burn Illinois coal and send harmful gases deep into the ground.

GOODS FOR THE WORLD

Since the days of John Deere and Cyrus McCormick, manufacturing has been an important part of the Illinois economy. In recent years, some companies have moved their factories overseas, where wages are lower. But more than 800,000 people still earn their paychecks in Illinois by making products for others to use.

Farm equipment is still made in Illinois, with the Deere Company leading the way. Today, the company

WORD TO KNOW

genetic engineering *changing genes, the chemicals in plants and animals that determine the traits passed from one generation to the next*

SEE IT HERE!

LONG GROVE CONFECTIONERY COMPANY

The Chicago area is said by many to be the candy capital of the world. Today, some companies in the region still produce chocolate and other sweets. If you head to Buffalo Grove, you can watch the folks at the Long Grove Confectionary Company making their delicious candies. See workers making chocolates by hand, and get a whiff of the huge sculpture—made from more than a ton of chocolate! And of course, visitors top off their tour by tasting samples.

John Deere founded makes tractors of all sizes and farm implements, for raising crops or cutting suburban lawns. Another notable manufacturer is Caterpillar, which makes equipment used for heavy-duty jobs such as construction, mining, and power generation. Automakers are also represented in the state, with Ford and Chrysler building vehicles at plants in Chicago and Belvidere.

Not all Illinois manufactured goods roll on wheels and are made of steel. Illinois companies make a wide range of chemical products, especially medicines. **Pharmaceutical** companies in the state rely on highly trained scientists who explore what makes people sick and how to make them well.

WORD TO KNOW

pharmaceutical *relating to the manufacture and sale of drugs used in medicine*

A John Deere harvester collects wheat from an Illinois field.

ALL SORTS OF SERVICE

Whether it's ringing up sales at a cash register or stitching up a nasty cut in an emergency room, Illinoisans work in a variety of jobs that are part of the service industry. The service industry includes retail stores. Sears Holdings Corporation, one of the nation's largest retailers, is based in Hoffman Estates. Travel is also part of the service sector. United Airlines, one of the largest airlines in the world, is centered in Chicago.

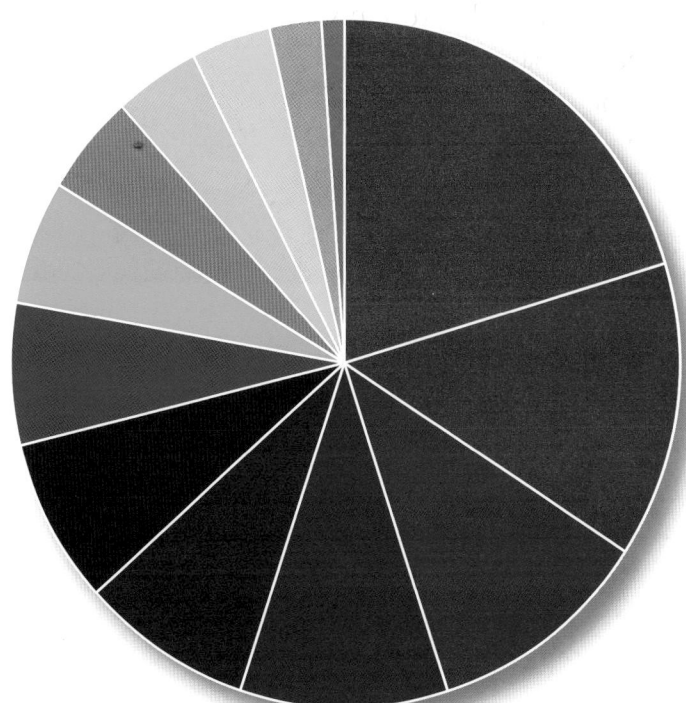

What Do Illinoisans Do?

This color-coded chart shows what industries Illinoisans work in.

20.5% Educational, health and social services, 1,218,536

13.7% Manufacturing, 815,406

10.8% Retail trade, 645,111

10.2% Professional, scientific, management, administrative, and waste management services, 607,321

8.1% Arts, entertainment, recreation, accommodation and food services, 481,011

8.0% Finance, insurance, real estate, and rental and leasing, 478,925

6.5% Construction, 385,129

5.9% Transportation and warehousing, and utilities, 353,672

4.8% Other services (except public administration), 286,238

4.0% Public administration, 236,127

3.9% Wholesale trade, 232,523

2.5% Information, 149,259

1.0% Agriculture, forestry, fishing and hunting, and mining, 62,096

Source: U.S. Census Bureau, 2005 estimate

Traders at the Chicago Mercantile Exchange. Those in the upper left are traders in NASDAQ; those in the foreground trade for the S&P 500.

WORD TO KNOW

commodities *goods such as minerals and farm products*

Services also include financial activities, such as insurance, banking, and buying and selling stock and **commodities**. Two of the top insurance companies in the United States have headquarters in Illinois. Chicago is one of the top financial cities in the United States. At the Chicago Board of Trade (CBOT) and Chicago Mercantile Exchange (CME), brokers buy and sell contracts for a variety of commodities, including crops, livestock, and metals such as gold and silver. In 2006, the CME and CBOT announced plans to merge, creating the largest company of its kind in the world!

Chicago is also home to a number of notable publishing companies. The Johnson Publishing Company was founded by John H. Johnson in 1942 to target African American readers. Today, Johnson Publishing is the largest African American–owned publishing company in the United States. Its popular products include *Ebony* and *Jet* magazines. The company is now run by the founder's daughter, Linda Johnson Rice.

The service industry isn't all serious business. It includes entertainment, too, and once again Chicago is the place to go in Illinois for television, music, and other forms of entertainment. Chicago theaters attract tourists from across the Midwest. Film companies often go to the city—and other spots in Illinois—to make movies. Some recent examples are *Spider-Man II*, *Barbershop*, and *Batman Begins*. In 2004, entertainment companies provided jobs for about 15,000 people.

No matter what the industry, Illinois is a vibrant place for people to make a living.

OPRAH WINFREY: BILLIONAIRE BUSINESSWOMAN

When you think of talk shows, you probably think of Oprah Winfrey (1954–). Born in Mississippi, she went to Chicago in 1984 to host a morning TV talk show. Chatting with guests about a wide range of issues, from politics to health, she became a hit. *The Oprah Winfrey Show* went national in 1986. From there, Winfrey branched out into acting, producing, and publishing, building a business empire worth more than $1 billion. She shares her wealth by sometimes giving her guests and charities generous gifts. One of her projects is a private school for girls in South Africa, which opened in early 2007.

Spider-Man II, starring Tobey Maguire, is one of the many movies that have been filmed on the streets of Chicago.

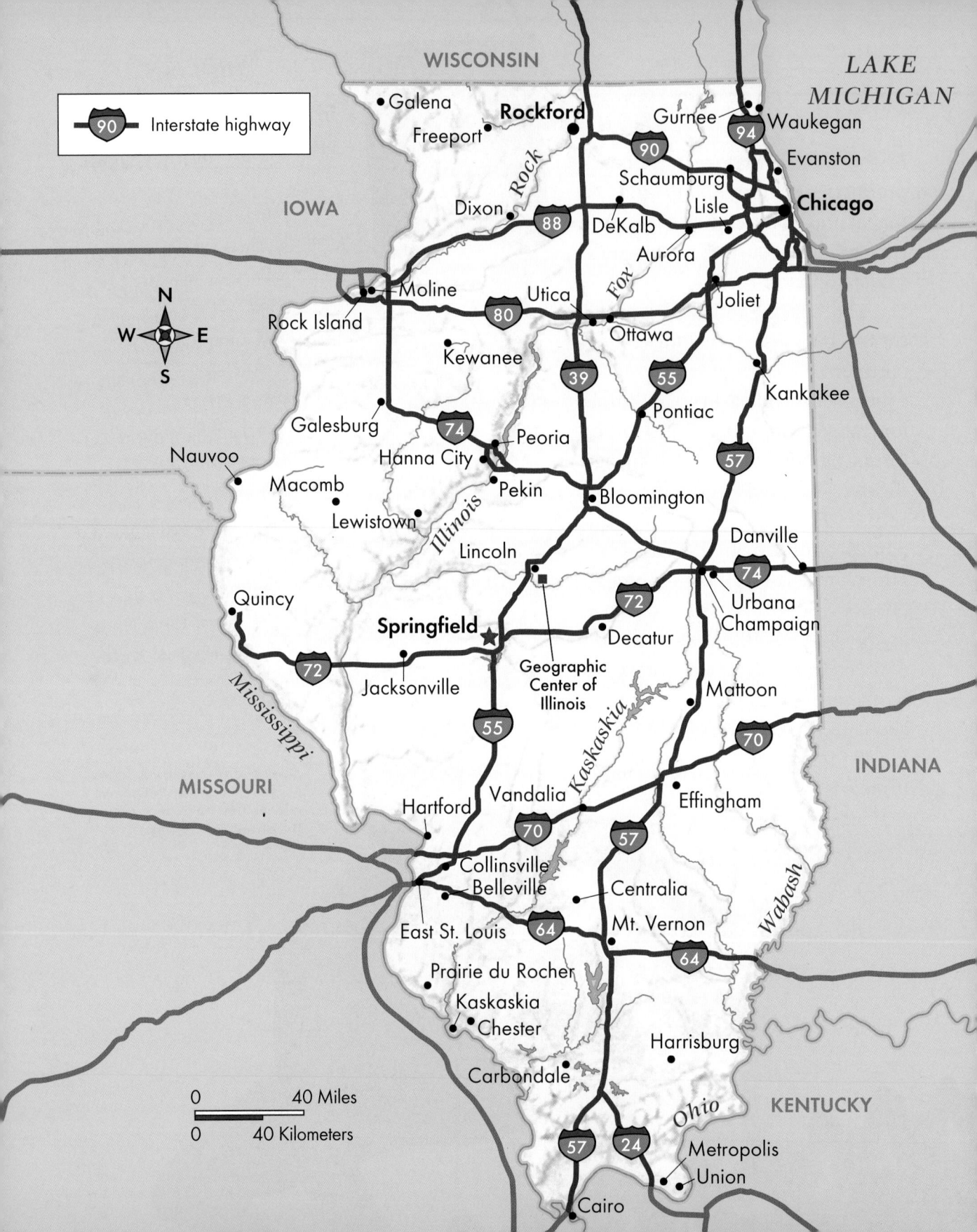

CHAPTER NINE

TRAVEL GUIDE

TRAVEL GUIDE

★

FROM THE STRIKING LAKEFRONT OF THE WINDY CITY TO THE HISTORIC CAPITAL OF SPRINGFIELD AND THE SOUTHERN PLAINS, ILLINOIS HAS MUCH TO SEE. Take a trip to Springfield and learn more about Abe Lincoln; stop by Chicago and take in a baseball game at historic Wrigley Field. Visit the Shedd Aquarium or spend a day hiking through Shawnee National Forest. You've read all about it—now grab your map, and let's go!

← Follow along with this travel map. We'll begin up north in Chicago and travel all the way south to Chester!

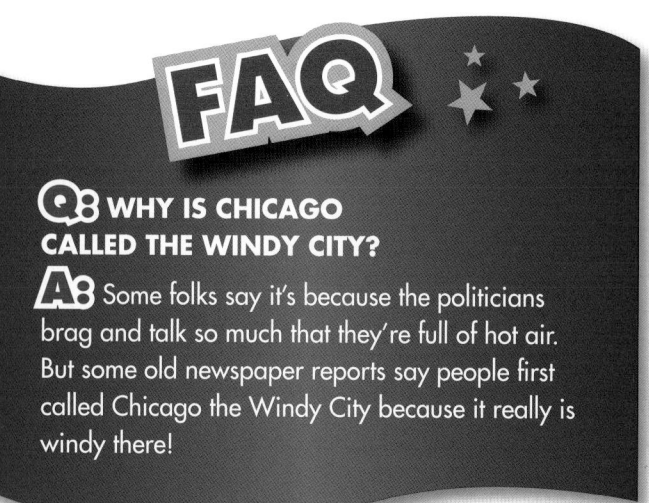

FAQ

Q: WHY IS CHICAGO CALLED THE WINDY CITY?

A: Some folks say it's because the politicians brag and talk so much that they're full of hot air. But some old newspaper reports say people first called Chicago the Windy City because it really is windy there!

CHICAGOLAND

THINGS TO DO: Climb 110 stories to the top of the Sears Tower, bike ride along the lakefront, or visit the world's most complete *Tyrannosaurus rex* skeleton, Sue.

Chicago

★ **Navy Pier:** This popular tourist attraction features the Chicago Children's Museum, an IMAX theater, and the Chicago Shakespeare Theater. Outside you can take a ride on the 15-story Ferris wheel or enjoy Wednesday-night fireworks during the summer!

★ **Millennium Park:** This wondrous 4.5-acre (9.9-ha) park is a showplace for the arts. Catch an outdoor concert at the state-of-the-art Jay Pritzker Pavilion, take a leisurely stroll through the park grounds, or visit "the Bean"—a 110-ton steel sculpture. Ice-skating is offered in the winter and free exercise classes every Saturday in the summer.

★ **Lincoln Park Zoo:** Located in the middle of the city, this is one of the oldest public zoos in the country. Get up close and personal with a gorilla in the Regenstein Center for African apes, hear the lions roar, and paddle along the lagoon in a swan boat. Open every day and always free!

The Ferris wheel at Navy Pier

Sue, the *T. Rex* at the Field Museum

★ **Sears Tower:** Enjoy the panoramic view from atop the nation's tallest building! The Sears Tower Skydeck features interactive exhibits that map out the city's landmarks, as well as high-powered telescopes for a bird's-eye view of the magnificent city below.

★ **The Field Museum:** From ancient Egyptian artifacts to Native American and African cultural exhibits, the Field Museum has something for everyone. Don't forget to say hello to the world's most complete *T. rex* skeleton affectionately named Sue!

★ **John G. Shedd Aquarium:** After hitting the Field Museum, walk next door to the amazing Shedd Aquarium. From lizards to sharks to stingrays and dolphins, the Shedd Aquarium is a must-see for any lover of marine animal life!

SEE IT HERE!

EXPLORING THE WORLD OF SCIENCE AND INDUSTRY

Want to see what it's like inside a coal mine or learn about a record-setting train? Then Chicago's Museum of Science and Industry is the place to be. The museum is located along Lake Michigan in the only surviving building from the 1893 Columbian Exposition. Visitors can take an elevator down to an exhibit that shows how coal is mined and step onto the Pioneer Zephyr, which made a nonstop train trip from Denver to Chicago in 1934.

★ **Adler Planetarium & Astronomy Museum:** Star light, star bright, go visit the Adler Planetarium tonight! While you're there, check out the renowned Sky Theater. Put your head back and watch as the ceiling of this domed theater turns into a star-filled night sky. See the Milky Way, learn to recognize the constellations, and marvel at the farthest reaches of the universe!

★ **The Art Institute of Chicago:** One of the world's leading art museums houses works by some of the greatest artists in history, ranging from impressionist Claude Monet to pop artist Andy Warhol.

ROUTE 66

Route 66 was the name of a 1940s song and a 1960s TV show. But first it was a highway that began in downtown Chicago and headed west to Los Angeles. Along the way, the route passed through many small towns, giving them their first major road link to other parts of the country. Route 66 was sometimes called the Main Street of America. But by the 1980s, it was no longer a national highway. The state of Illinois has put up signs showing where Route 66 once ran, so travelers can explore the highway and visit the truck stops and diners along the way.

White Sox baseball cap

★ **Baseball:** Chicago is a huge sports town, so it's no surprise that it's also home to two Major League Baseball teams. Visit historic Wrigley Field on the North Side to cheer on the Chicago Cubs, or visit the 2005 World Series Champion Chicago White Sox at U.S. Cellular Field on the South Side.

Gurnee

★ **Six Flags Great America/ Hurricane Harbor:** Soar like a superhero on the Superman: Ultimate Flight roller coaster. Catch your breath, then chug along the Scenic Railway or catch a colorful stage show at Six Flags Great America theme park. When you're ready to cool off, head over to the Hurricane Harbor Water Park!

Lisle

★ **The Morton Arboretum:** Home to 1,700 acres (688 ha) of spectacular gardens, this site holds a world-renowned plant collection and unique natural areas that can be viewed by car, on foot, or via the open-air Acorn Express tram.

Wrigley Field

NORTHERN

THINGS TO DO: Visit the homes of former U.S. presidents Ulysses S. Grant and Ronald Reagan, take a walk through the Anderson Japanese Gardens, or enjoy a symphony recital at the extravagant Coronado Theatre!

Rockford

★ **Anderson Japanese Gardens:** Stroll through the lush gardens of the Anderson Japanese Gardens, where you will discover crystal clear waterfalls, koi ponds, and a teahouse built in the classic Sukiya style of architecture!

★ **Coronado Theatre:** The Coronado Theatre is an architectural masterpiece. The interior incorporates influences from Spanish castles to Italian villas. Originally built as a movie palace and vaudeville hall, today, it is a great place to enjoy classical music.

★ **Burpee Museum of Natural History:** No, this is not a belching museum! This museum houses a bevy of exhibits ranging from Native American full-sized wigwams and tepees, to a two-story coal forest and a 21-foot (6.4-m) dinosaur skeleton named Jane.

Koi

★ **Discovery Center Museum:** Calling all scientists and techies! In this museum of science and technology, navigate your way through a robotics lab, an art studio, and an air and flight museum that will take your breath away! There is no shortage of fun at this museum, and there is something for everyone.

Utica

★ **Starved Rock State Park:** Hike through lush forests and explore canyons and sparkling waterfalls in a spectacular setting along the Illinois River!

Union

★ **Illinois Railway Museum:** Train buffs make tracks to the Illinois Railway Museum, the largest railway museum in the country. More than 250 railcars and locomotives are on display, including a complete Burlington Zephyr Streamliner. All aboard!

Burlington Zephyr Streamliner

Home of Ulysses S. Grant

Galena

★ **Ulysses S. Grant Home State Historic Site:** This beautifully furnished home was presented to General Grant as a gift for the returning Civil War hero. Visit this historic home to catch a glimpse of early life in Illinois!

★ **Main Street:** This historic district stays in touch with its 19th-century roots. In fact, 85 percent of Galena is registered as an historic place. Visit charming shops, restaurants, bistros, and landmark buildings. Truly a blast from the past and an Illinois gem!

Dixon

★ **Ronald Reagan Home and Visitor Center:** Come take a tour of the boyhood home of one of America's most charismatic presidents. This home has been restored to its 1920s state, complete with decor and furniture from the period.

CENTRAL

THINGS TO DO: Browse the expansive Abraham Lincoln Presidential Library, visit the Illinois State Capitol, or catch a Big Ten Conference basketball game at the University of Illinois—home of the Fightin' Illini.

Springfield

★ **Abraham Lincoln Presidential Library and Museum:** This is the largest presidential museum in the nation, featuring an extensive collection of artifacts

Abraham Lincoln hologram

and memorabilia from the Civil War. A special-effects exhibit retells Lincoln's history through holographic "ghosts."

★ **Lincoln Home National Historic Site:** Visit the historic home where Abraham Lincoln and his wife, Mary Todd Lincoln, lived when he served as a prominent lawyer in Springfield.

Home of Abraham Lincoln

★ **Lincoln-Herndon Law Offices State Historic Site:** See where Abraham Lincoln worked before he became president. It was here that he began his career as a great lawyer, which would eventually catapult him all the way to the White House!

★ **Lincoln Tomb State Historic Site:** Pay respects to our 16th president, Abraham Lincoln. This solemn site is the final resting place of the great president, and pays homage to him and all of those who lost their lives in the Civil War.

★ **Illinois State Capitol:** Observe a live session of the Illinois legislature, and see what important decisions are being made in the Land of Lincoln. Nearby you can also visit the original building that housed the state capitol.

SEE IT HERE!

THE DANA-THOMAS HOUSE

In Springfield, fans of architect Frank Lloyd Wright can explore the Dana-Thomas House, one of the best surviving examples of the Prairie style of architecture. Wright designed buildings that matched the level, open spaces of the prairie. Roofs are low and flat, and inside, the living spaces flow together, instead of being cut off by walls. The Dana-Thomas House, a state historic site, was completed in 1904. Visitors can see more than 100 pieces of furniture that Wright also designed for the home, along with hundreds of original windows, doors, and light fixtures.

Urbana

★ **University of Illinois:** Take a tour of the University of Illinois. Catch a Fightin' Illini basketball game at Assembly Hall.

Decatur

★ **Scovill Zoo:** Located on a bluff overlooking Lake Decatur, the Scovill Zoo features more than 400 animals! Jump on a train, but be sure to stop by the Oriental gardens, the Children's Museum of Illinois, and the endangered species carousel.

University of Illinois at Urbana

Lemur

WESTERN

THINGS TO DO: Visit a farmer's heaven at the John Deere Pavilion, pay homage to the Sauk and Fox Indian tribes at Black Hawk State Historic Site, and view black bears, wolves, and cougars in their natural habitat at the Wildlife Prairie State Park.

MINI-BIO

JOHN DEERE: FROM BLACKSMITH TO ENTREPRENEUR

John Deere (1804–1886) never dreamed that he would one day become an entrepreneur of a thriving company. Born into poverty in Vermont, Deere was 17 when he headed to the Midwest to work as an apprentice blacksmith. One day, in 1817, Deere spotted a broken saw blade in the corner of a sawmill and asked the owner if he could take it back to his shop. There he fashioned the world's first successful steel plow, which would allow farmers all over to more easily plow their land. Deere's early success became a successful farming equipment company.

Moline

★ **John Deere Pavilion:** This pavilion celebrates the life and innovation of the man who revolutionized agricultural farming forever. The John Deere Pavilion features interactive agricultural sites, vintage and antique farming equipment, and a John Deere souvenir shop!

Nauvoo

★ **Nauvoo Temple:** A reconstructed version of the original Mormon temple, this building is an architectural beauty. Although it is not open to the public, the view of the exterior of the building is thrilling in itself. If you're passing through Nauvoo, this landmark is worth a stop.

Hanna City

★ **Wildlife Prairie State Park:** Journey through this 2,000-acre (809-ha) zoological park and see native animals such as cougars, bison, wolves, and black bears in their natural habitat. Learn about the frontier days at the Pioneer Farmstead, and see an original one-room schoolhouse and log cabin on the grounds.

Bison

Galesburg

★ **Carl Sandburg Historic Site:**
Visit the birthplace and grave of
the Pulitzer Prize–winning writer,
poet, and Lincoln biographer.
Learn more about Carl Sandburg
and his influence on Illinois and in
the nation.

Lewistown

★ **Dickson Mounds Museum:** An
archaeological treasure, this is one
of the major on-site archaeological
museums in the country. It special-
izes in the archaeological history
of the American Indian and the
Illinois River Valley.

Cave-in-Rock State Park

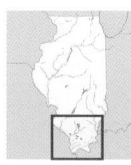

SOUTHERN

THINGS TO DO: Hike through
a scenic national forest or
strike a superhero pose with
Superman!

Harrisburg

★ **Shawnee National Forest:** The
only national forest in Illinois, it
is great for outdoor adventures.
Explore the forest on horseback, or
take a hike and marvel at the rock
formations in the Garden of the
Gods and Cave-in-Rock State Park.

SEE IT HERE!

A CAVE FOR CROOKS

Along Illinois's bank of the Ohio River is a mammoth
cave called Cave-in-Rock. It's 55 feet (17 m) high, 20
feet (6 m) wide, and 200 feet (61 m) deep. More than
200 years ago, Cave-in-Rock was a hideout for various
pirates and criminals. In 1797, Samuel Mason hung a
sign outside the cave advertising a tavern. When thirsty
travelers on the Ohio stopped in for a drink, Mason and
his thugs robbed and killed them. A few years later, two
murderers known as the Harpe Brothers hid in the cave
while running from the law. Today, Cave-in-Rock is part
of an Illinois state park of the same name.

Metropolis
(Home of Superman)

★ **Fort Massac State Park:** Calling all history buffs! Illinois's first state park features a replica of the 1802 Fort Massac, as well as Native American and military artifacts on site. Guides are on site to explain the history and significance behind the fort.

★ **Superman Statue:** He stands for truth, justice, and the American way—he's Superman! DC Comics gave Metropolis the permission to proclaim itself the official home of Superman. Visitors from all over the world come to pose with this enormous superhero!

SEE IT HERE!

A SUPER PLACE TO VISIT

In the comic book, Superman lives in Metropolis, though the state is not named. Residents of Metropolis, Illinois, decided their town should be Superman's hometown, and the creators of Superman agreed. Now Metropolis is the home of the Super Museum and an annual Superman Celebration. The museum has the largest collection of Superman gear in the world. The celebration draws stars who have appeared in different Superman movies and TV shows.

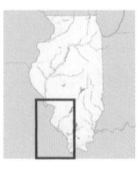

SOUTHWEST

THINGS TO DO: Follow in the footsteps of American explorers Lewis and Clark, meditate at the largest outdoor shrine in the country, or visit the world-renowned Cahokia Indian Mounds.

Hartford

★ **Lewis and Clark Interpretive Center:** Walk along the east bank of the Mississippi River, where the Corps of Discovery, under Lewis and Clark, launched their epic journey. The Interpretive Center tells the story of Camp River DuBois, the original encampment and training grounds of Lewis and Clark, and includes a full-scale replica of the team's keelboat.

Belleville

★ **National Shrine of Our Lady of the Snows:** The nation's largest outdoor shrine is dedicated to maintaining a peaceful, outdoor environment for private meditation, reflection, and prayer. A peaceful spot for an afternoon stroll or period of reflection!

SEE IT HERE!
WHAT A SIGHT

Driving through Collinsville, it's hard to miss this really red sight—the world's largest bottle of ketchup! Collinsville was once the home of a company that made different kinds of food, including ketchup. The company is gone, but the water tower that looks like a ketchup bottle remains. Many people consider the 170-foot-tall (52-m) bottle (right) a piece of roadside art.

Collinsville

★ **Cahokia Mounds:** This U.N. World Heritage Site hosts the remains of an ancient city where a Mississippian Indian culture once flourished. Sixty-eight of the original 120 earthen mounds have been preserved on the 4,000-acre (1,619-ha) site. Check out the 100-foot (30-m)-tall Monks Mound, which is the largest prehistoric earthen mound in the world.

East St. Louis

★ **Eads Bridge:** This magnificent structure was built in 1874 to cross the Mississippi River and link St. Louis, Missouri, to Illinois. At that time, it was the longest arch bridge in the world, with an overall length of 6,442 feet (1,964 m).

Chester

★ **Popeye Statue:** Elzie C. Segar, the creator of Popeye the cartoon, was born in Chester. Come pay homage to the famous cartoon sailor.

WRITING PROJECTS

Check out these ideas for creating travel brochures and writing you-are-there editorials. Or learn about the state quarter and design your own.

118

ART PROJECTS

119

You can act out interviews with famous people from the state, illustrate the state song, or create a great PowerPoint presentation.

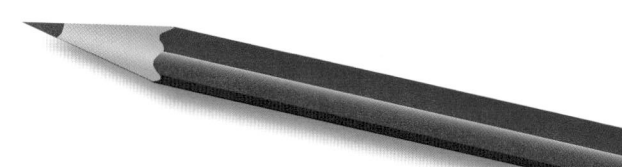

TIMELINE

What happened when? This timeline highlights important events in the state's history—and shows what was happening throughout the United States at the same time.

122

FAST FACTS

126

Use this section to find fascinating facts about state symbols, land area and population statistics, weather, sports teams, and much more.

GLOSSARY

125

Remember the Words to Know from the chapters in this book? They're all collected here.

SCIENCE, TECHNOLOGY, & MATH PROJECTS

Make weather maps, learn about population statistics, and research famous inventors from the state.

PRIMARY VS. SECONDARY SOURCES

So what are primary and secondary sources and what's the diff? This section explains all that and where you can find them.

BIOGRAPHICAL DICTIONARY

This at-a-glance guide highlights some of the state's most important and influential people. Visit this section and read up about their contributions to the state, the country, and the world.

RESOURCES

Books, Web sites, DVDs, and more. Take a look at these additional sources for information about the state.

WRITING PROJECTS

★ ★ ★

Create an Election Brochure or Web Site!

Run for office!

Throughout this book, you've read about some of the issues that concern Illinois today.

★ As a candidate for governor of Illinois, create a campaign brochure or Web site.

★ Talk about the three or four major issues you'll focus on if you are elected.

★ Remember, you'll be responsible for Illinois's budget. How would you spend the taxpayers' money?

SEE: Chapter 7, pages 81–91.

GO TO: Illinois's Government Web site at www.illinois.gov. You can learn about what it takes to run the state.

State Quarter Project

From 1999 to 2008, the U.S. Mint introduced new quarters commemorating each of the 50 states in the order that they were admitted to the Union. Each state's quarter features a unique design on its back, or reverse.

GO TO: www.quarterdesigns.com/index.html and find out what's featured on the back of the Illinois quarter.

★ Research the significance of each image. Who designed the quarter? Who chose the final design?

★ Design your own Illinois quarter. What images would you choose for the reverse?

★ Make a poster showing the Illinois quarter and label each image.

Write a Memoir, Journal, or Editorial for Your School Newspaper!

Picture Yourself . . .

★ Growing up as a teenager in an Illiniwek village.
    SEE: Chapter 2, page 24.

★ Living on the Illinois frontier of the 18th century, blending the cultures of three peoples: French, Indian, and African.
    SEE: Chapter 3, pages 32–33.

★ On an expedition with Canadian trapper Louis Jolliet and missionary Jacques Marquette. You sail from Canada, across Lake Michigan, and down the Fox and Wisconsin rivers to the Mississippi. Describe what you see, and your encounters with local people.
    SEE: Chapter 3, page 29.

★ Working with René-Robert Cavelier, Sieur de la Salle, to set up forts in the Illinois territory. Describe the challenges you face and how you overcome them.
    SEE: Chapter 3, page 31.

Louis Jolliet and Jacques Marquette on the Mississippi River

ART PROJECTS

★ ★ ★

Create a PowerPoint Presentation or Visitors' Guide

Welcome to Illinois!

Illinois is a great place to visit, and to live! From its natural beauty to its bustling cities and historic sites, there's plenty to see and do. In your PowerPoint presentation or brochure, highlight 10 to 15 of Illinois's amazing landmarks. Be sure to include:

★ a map of the state showing where these sites are located

★ photos, illustrations, Web links, natural history facts, geographic stats, climate and weather, plants and wildlife, and recent discoveries.

SEE: Chapter 9, pages 104–115.

GO TO: The official Web site of Illinois tourism at www.enjoyillinois.com/. Download and print maps, photos, national landmark images, and vacationing ideas for tourists.

Illustrate the Lyrics to the Illinois State Song ("Illinois")

★ Use markers, paints, photos, collage, colored pencils, or computer graphics to illustrate the lyrics to "Illinois," the state song! Turn your illustrations into a picture book, or scan them into a PowerPoint and add music!

SEE: The lyrics to "Illinois" on page 128.

GO TO: The Illinois state Web site at www.Illinois. gov to find out more about the origin of the Illinois state song, "Illinois."

Be Oprah for a Day!

Gather up a pen, a notepad, and a friend. Look online to see what you can find out about some of the famous people you have learned about in this book, including Sandra Cisneros, Richard M. Daley, Abraham Lincoln, Barack Obama, and many more. Then, with a friend, script and perform an interview with that person and present it to your class. Feeling brave? Take questions from your "audience" and get their input about what made your interviewee so famous!

SEE: Chapters 6 and 7, pages 66–91.

GO TO: The Chicago History Museum Web site at www.chicagohs.org to find out more about famous public figures in Chicago and Illinois.

Oprah Winfrey

SCIENCE, TECHNOLOGY, & MATH PROJECTS

Graph Population Statistics!

★ Compare population statistics (such as ethnic background, birth, death, and literacy rates) in Illinois counties or major cities.

★ In your graph or chart, look at population density and write sentences describing what the population statistics show; graph one set of population statistics and write a paragraph explaining what the graphs reveal.

SEE: Chapter 6, pages 68–72.

GO TO: The official Web site for the U.S. Census Bureau at www.census.gov, and at http://quickfacts.census.gov/qfd/ to find out more about population statistics, how they work, and what the statistics are for Illinois.

Create a Weather Map of Illinois!

Use your knowledge of Illinois's geography to research and identify conditions that result in specific weather events, including thunderstorms and tornadoes. What is it about the geography of Illinois that makes it vulnerable to things like tornadoes? Create a weather map or poster that shows the weather patterns over the state. To accompany your map, explain the technology used to measure weather phenomena and provide data.

SEE: Chapter 1, pages 13–14.

GO TO: The National Oceanic and Atmospheric Administration's National Weather Service Web site at www.weather.gov for weather maps and forecasts for Illinois.

Learn About Illinois Inventions

Many great inventors have come from Illinois. Farming wouldn't be what it is without John Deere's plows or Cyrus McCormick's reapers. Research other great inventions and do a report on your favorite. How has it changed the world? What would make the invention even better? Put your scientific mind to work!

SEE: Chapters 4, 8, and 9, pages 44–45, 99–100, and 112.

McCormick reaper

PRIMARY VS. SECONDARY SOURCES

★ ★ ★

What's the Diff?

Your teacher may require at least one or two primary sources and one or two secondary sources for your assignment. So, what's the difference between the two?

★ **PRIMARY sources are original.** You are reading the actual words of someone's diary, journal, letter, autobiography, or interview. Primary sources can also be photographs, maps, prints, cartoons, news/film footage, posters, first-person newspaper articles, drawings, musical scores, and recordings. By the way, when you conduct a survey, interview someone, shoot a video or take photographs to include in a project—you are creating primary sources!

★ **SECONDARY sources are what you find in encyclopedias, textbooks, articles, biographies, and almanacs**. These are written by a person or group of people who tell about something that happened to someone else. Secondary sources also recount what another person said or did. This book is an example of a secondary source.

Now that you know what primary sources are—where can you find them?

★ **Your school or local library:** Check the library catalog for collections of original writings, government documents, musical scores, and so on. Some of this material may be stored on microfilm. The Library of Congress Web site (www.loc.gov) is an excellent online resource for primary source materials.

★ **Historical societies:** These organizations keep historical documents, photographs, and other materials. Staff members can help you find what you are looking for. History museums are also great places to see primary sources first-hand.

★ **The Internet:** There are lots of Web sites that have primary sources you can download and use in a project or assignment.

Letter from Abraham Lincoln, 1864

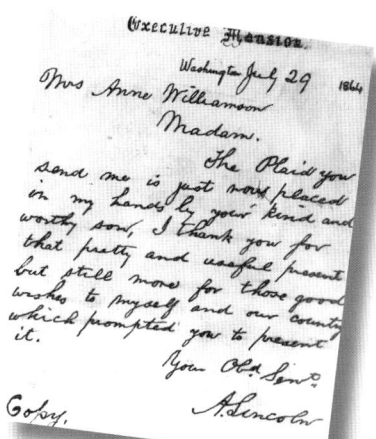

TIMELINE

★ ★ ★

U.S. Events	1500	Illinois Events

1500s
The Illiniwek begin to settle in Illinois.

1565
Spanish admiral Pedro Menéndez de Avilés founds St. Augustine, Florida, the oldest continuously occupied European settlement in the continental United States.

1600

1671
France claims the Illinois country.

1673
Louis Jolliet and Jacques Marquette explore Illinois.

1680
The French build their first fort in Illinois.

1682
René-Robert Cavelier, Sieur de La Salle, claims more than 1 million square miles (2.6 million sq km) of territory in the Mississippi River basin for France, naming it Louisiana.

1700

1703
The French found the settlement of Kaskaskia.

c. 1720
The first African slaves are brought to Illinois.

1755–63
England and France fight over North American colonial lands in the French and Indian War. By the end of the war, France has ceded all of its land west of the Mississippi to Spain and its Canadian territories to England.

1763
Great Britain receives Illinois from France.

1765
British forces arrive at Fort de Chartres to take formal control of Illinois.

1776
Thirteen American colonies declare their independence from Britain, marking the beginning of the Revolutionary War.

1778–79
U.S. forces led by George Rogers Clark take control of several forts in the Illinois country.

1779
Jean-Baptiste Pointe du Sable builds a trading post in Chicago.

1783
The United States officially gains control of Illinois from Great Britain.

U.S. Events

Illinois Events

1787
The U.S. Constitution is written.

1787
Illinois becomes part of the Northwest Territory, with its capital at Kaskaskia.

1795
The Treaty of Greenville ends fighting between U.S. forces and several Indian tribes; the tribes turn over lands in Illinois to the Americans.

1800

George Rogers Clark on the way to Kaskaskia

1818
Illinois approves its first constitution and enters the Union as the 21st state.

1830
The Indian Removal Act forces eastern Native American groups to relocate west of the Mississippi River.

1832
The Americans win the Black Hawk War, the last Indian war fought in Illinois.

1837
Springfield becomes the capital of Illinois.

1846–48
The United States fights a war with Mexico over western territories in the Mexican War.

1848
The Illinois and Michigan Canal is completed, linking the Great Lakes with the Mississippi River.

1858
Stephen Douglas and Abraham Lincoln hold a series of debates across Illinois.

1860
Lincoln is elected president, leading to the Civil War.

1861–65
The American Civil War is fought between the Northern Union and the Southern Confederacy; it ends with the surrender of the Confederate Army, led by General Robert E. Lee.

1871
A huge fire destroys a large part of Chicago.

1886
Apache leader Geronimo surrenders to the U.S. Army, ending the last major Native American rebellion against the expansion of the United States into the West.

1889
Jane Addams opens Hull-House to help immigrants adjust to life in Chicago.

1893
Chicago hosts the World's Columbian Exposition, where the first Ferris wheel is used.

U.S. Events 1900 Illinois Events

1910s

The Great Migration of African Americans from the rural South to the North almost triples the black population of Chicago.

1917-18

The United States is engaged in World War I.

1929

The stock market crashes, plunging the United States into the Great Depression.

1931

As the Great Depression nears its peak, 1.1 million Illinoisans are out of work.

1941- 45

The United States engages in World War II.

1942

Scientists at the University of Chicago produce the first controlled atomic reaction, which leads to the development of the first nuclear weapons.

1954

The U.S. Supreme Court prohibits segregation of public schools in the *Brown v. Board of Education* ruling.

1968

Mayor Richard J. Daley orders Chicago police to attack antiwar protesters at the Democratic National Convention.

1973

Work finishes on Chicago's Sears Tower, the tallest building in the United States.

1980

Illinois native Ronald Reagan is elected U.S. president.

Oprah Winfrey

1986

Oprah Winfrey airs her Chicago-based TV talk show across the United States.

1991

The United States and other nations join the brief Persian Gulf War against Iraq.

1996

Illinois introduces teen courts, in which teens set punishments for their peers.

2000

2001

Terrorists hijack four U.S. aircraft and crash them into the World Trade Center in New York City, the Pentagon in Washington, D.C., and a Pennsylvania field, killing thousands.

2006

Rod Blagojevich wins his second term as governor of Illinois.

2009

Scheduled opening of the 1,362-foot-tall (415-m) Trump Tower.

GLOSSARY

★   ★   ★

abolitionists people who were opposed to slavery and worked to end it

allies friends or supporters, especially during wartime

archaeologists scientists who study the items left behind by ancient peoples

candidate a person who runs for a political office

commodities goods such as minerals and farm products

confederation a union of several political or social groups

genetic engineering changing genes, the chemicals in plants and animals that determine the traits passed from one generation to the next

Industrial Revolution the rapid growth of factories and use of large machines to produce goods that began in England in the 18th century

invasive species wildlife that is not native to a region and harms native plants or animals

mercenaries soldiers who will fight for any army willing to pay them

missionary a priest, minister, or other deeply religious person who tries to convince others to practice a certain religion

nuclear weapon a bomb that uses the huge amount of power stored inside the atoms of some materials to create large explosions

ordinances laws passed by local governments

peers people of a similar age or background

pharmaceutical relating to the manufacture and sale of drugs used in medicine

prejudice an unreasonable hatred or fear of others

receded pulled or moved back over time

shamans spiritual leaders who had powers to cure the sick and influence events

sponsor to act as a person who proposes or creates a bill

strike to refuse to work, as a sign of protest

unions organizations formed by workers to try to improve working conditions and wages

FAST FACTS

★ ★ ★

State Symbols

Statehood date	December 3, 1818, the 21st state
Origin of state name	French word; *Illiniwek* is an Algonquin word meaning "the men" or "tribe of superior men"
State capital	Springfield
State nickname	The Prairie State
State motto	"State Sovereignty, National Union"
State bird	Cardinal
State animal	White-tailed deer
State flower	Violet
State fish	Bluegill
State insect	Monarch butterfly
State mineral	Fluorite
State song	"Illinois" (See p. 128 for lyrics)
State tree	White oak
State fair	Springfield, mid-August

State seal

Geography

Total area; rank	57,914 square miles (149,997 sq km); 25th
Land; rank	55,584 square miles (143,963 sq km); 24th
Water; rank	2,331 square miles (6,037 sq km); 20th
Inland water	756 square miles (1,958 sq km); 28th
Great Lakes	1,575 square miles (4,079 sq km); 6th
Geographic center	In Logan County, 28 miles (45 km) northeast of Springfield
Latitude and Longitude	36° 58′ N to 42° 30′ N 87° 30′ W to 91° 30′ W
Highest point	Charles Mound, 1,235 feet (376 m)
Lowest point	279 feet (85 m) at the Mississippi River
Largest city	Chicago
Number of counties	102
Longest river	Illinois River, 273 miles (439 km)

A little
blue heron

Population

Population; rank (2006 estimate)	12,831,970; 6th
Density (2006 estimate)	222 persons per square mile (86 per sq km)
Population distribution (2000 census)	88% urban, 12% rural
Race (2005 estimate)	White persons: 79.4%
	Black persons: 15.1%*
	Asian persons: 4.1%*
	American Indian and Alaska Native persons: 0.3%*
	Native Hawaiian and Other Pacific Islanders: 0.1%*
	Persons reporting two or more races: 1.1%
	Persons of Hispanic or Latino origin: 14.3%†
	White persons not Hispanic: 65.8%

Includes persons reporting only one race.
† Hispanics may be of any race, so are also included in applicable race categories.

Weather

Record high temperature	117°F (47°C) at East St. Louis on July 14, 1954
Record low temperature	−36°F (−38°C) at Congerville on January 5, 1999
Average July temperature	73°F (23°C)
Average January temperature	22°F (−6°C)
Average yearly precipitation	36.3 in. (92.2 cm)

State flag

STATE SONG

★ ★ ★

"Illinois"

Lyrics by C. H. Chamberlain; Music by Archibald Johnston

The words were written by C. H. Chamberlain, and the music was composed by Archibald Johnston. Johnston was active in the late 1800s and wrote other songs, such as "Baby Mine," "Our Little Daisy," and "Kiss Me, Would You?" In 1925, the 54th General Assembly enacted legislation that made "Illinois" the state song.

By thy rivers gently flowing, Illinois, Illinois,
O'er thy prairies verdant growing, Illinois, Illinois,
Comes an echo on the breeze.
Rustling through the leafy trees, and its mellow tones are these, Illinois, Illinois,
And its mellow tones are these, Illinois.

From a wilderness of prairies, Illinois, Illinois,
Straight thy way and never varies, Illinois, Illinois,
Till upon the inland sea,
Stands thy great commercial tree, turning all the world to thee, Illinois, Illinois,
Turning all the world to thee, Illinois.

When you heard your country calling, Illinois, Illinois,
Where the shot and shell were falling, Illinois, Illinois,
When the Southern host withdrew,
Pitting Gray against the Blue, There were none more brave than you, Illinois, Illinois,
There were none more brave than you, Illinois.

Not without thy wondrous story, Illinois, Illinois,
Can be writ the nation's glory, Illinois, Illinois,
On the record of thy years,
Abraham Lincoln's name appears, Grant and Logan, and our tears, Illinois, Illinois,
Grant and Logan, and our tears, Illinois.

NATURAL AREAS AND HISTORIC SITES

National Historic Sites

Lincoln Home National Historic Site was home to Abraham Lincoln before he became president.

National Historic Trails

Lewis and Clark National Historic Trail, *Mormon Pioneer Trail*, and *Trail of Tears National Historic Trail* each traverse parts of Illinois.

National Heritage Corridor

Illinois and Michigan National Heritage Corridor contains the former canal route between Chicago and LaSalle-Peru.

National Forest

Shawnee National Forest covers about 277,506 acres (112,303 ha) in southernmost Illinois.

State Parks and Forests

The Illinois Department of Natural Resources manages more than 120 sites, including 5 state forests, 73 state parks, and 2 state marinas. The largest is *Pere Marquette State Park*, at the junction of the Mississippi and Illinois rivers.

Arboretum

Morton Arboretum (Lisle) contains an extensive variety of plant life and covers 1,700 acres (688 ha).

SPORTS TEAMS

NCAA Teams (Division I)

Bradley University *Braves*
Chicago State University *Cougars*
DePaul University *Blue Demons*
Eastern Illinois University *Panthers*
Illinois State University *Redbirds*
Loyola University *Ramblers*
Northern Illinois University *Huskies*
Northwestern University *Wildcats*

Southern Illinois University *Salukis*
University of Illinois at Chicago *Flames*
University of Illinois at Urbana-Champaign
    Fighting Illini
Western Illinois University *Leathernecks*

PROFESSIONAL SPORTS TEAMS

Major League Baseball

Chicago Cubs
Chicago White Sox

Major League Soccer

Chicago Fire

National Basketball Association

Chicago Bulls

Women's National Basketball Association

Chicago Sky

National Football League

Chicago Bears

Arena Football League

Chicago Rush

National Hockey League

Chicago Blackhawks

CULTURAL INSTITUTIONS

★ ★ ★

Libraries

Chicago Public Library, opened in 1873, is the state's largest public library.

The Illinois State Historical Library (Springfield) has a substantial collection on Lincoln and Illinois history.

Museums

Abraham Lincoln Presidential Library and Museum (Springfield) houses one of the most diverse Lincoln and American Civil War collections in the United States.

Art Institute of Chicago is a world-class art museum housing extensive collections of the Masters and French Impressionists.

John G. Shedd Aquarium (Chicago) is home to a huge variety of aquatic life.

Adler Planetarium (Chicago) presents sky shows and houses astronomical artifacts.

Brookfield Zoo, officially the *Chicago Zoological Society,* is one of the nation's finest zoos. Visitors may see rare animals from all over the world.

Field Museum (Chicago), a natural science museum, houses more than 19 million artifacts and specimens.

Museum of Science and Industry (Chicago) is the largest tourist attraction in Illinois, drawing millions of visitors annually.

DuSable Museum of African American History (Chicago) chronicles the black experience in the United States.

Illinois State Museum (Springfield) was founded in 1877 and contains extensive collections on state history.

Performing Arts

Illinois has two major opera companies, three major symphony orchestras, and four major dance companies.

Universities and Colleges

In 2006, Illinois had 60 public and 99 private institutions of higher learning.

ANNUAL EVENTS

January–March

Chicago Boat, RV, & Outdoors Show at McCormick Place in Chicago (January)

Annual Groundhog Days in Woodstock (February)

Central Illinois Jazz Festival in Decatur (February)

Winter Carnival in Galena (February)

St. Patrick's Day Parade in Chicago (mid-March)

April–June

Old Capitol Art Fair in Springfield (late May)

Fort de Chartres Rendezvous in Prairie du Rocher (June)

Galena House Tours Festival (June)

Old Town Art Fair in Chicago (June)

The Steamboat Classic in Peoria (mid-June)

Taste of Chicago at Grant Park in Chicago (late June to early July)

Ravinia Music Festival in Highland Park (late June to mid-September)

July–September

Lisle Eyes to the Skies Balloon Festival (July)

Illinois State Fair in Springfield (August)

Lollapalooza Music Festival (August)

Chicago Jazz Festival (early September)

Du Quoin State Fair and World Trotting Derby (Labor Day weekend)

Grape Festival in Nauvoo (Labor Day weekend)

International Route 66 Mother Road Festival in Springfield (September–October)

October–December

Apple Festival in Long Grove (October)

Pumpkin Festival in Sycamore (October)

Scarecrow Festival in St. Charles (October)

Spoon River Scenic Drive Fall Festival in Fulton County (October)

International Folk Fair in Chicago (early November)

Christmas Around the World Display at the Museum of Science and Industry in Chicago (November–December)

Victorian Splendor Light Festival in Shelbyville (November to January)

BIOGRAPHICAL DICTIONARY

Robert Abbott (1870–1940) was the founder of the *Chicago Defender*, the African American newspaper that convinced many Southern blacks to move to the North.

Jane Addams See page 54.

Philip Armour (1832–1901) was a Chicago businessman who helped make the city the meat-butchering center of the United States.

Blue Balliett (1955–) is a children's author who was born in New York City but now lives in Chicago. Her books *Chasing Vermeer* and *The Wright 3* are set in Chicago.

Anna Pierce Hobbs Bigsby (1808–1869) was a doctor in southern Illinois who found a way to keep people safe from "milk sickness." When cows began getting sick and passing along their illness to humans, she discovered which plant was poisoning the cows.

Jesse Binga (1865–1950) was a successful Chicago-based African American banker and business owner.

Black Hawk See page 41.

Ray Bradbury (1920–) is a well-known science-fiction writer. He was born in Waukegan.

Carol Moseley Braun (1947–) is a Chicago lawmaker who in 1992 became the first African American woman elected to the U.S. Senate.

Gwendolyn Brooks (1917–2000) was a poet who was born in Kansas but moved to Chicago as a child. She won the Pulitzer Prize in 1950, the first African American to receive that honor.

Willa Beatrice Brown See page 58.

Edgar Rice Burroughs (1875–1950) was a writer best known for creating the Tarzan character. He was born in Chicago.

Dick Butkus See page 79.

Jane Byrne (1934–) was the first female mayor of Chicago.

Joseph Cannon (1836–1926) was a lawmaker who served as Speaker of the U.S. House of Representatives from 1903 to 1911. Called Uncle Joe, he was famous for his tight control of House affairs.

Edgar Rice Burroughs

Al Capone (1899–1947) was a notorious Chicago gangster known for his violent ways. He was a symbol for the lawlessness of Chicago during the 1920s.

Pat Charlebois See page 16.

Sandra Cisneros See page 75.

D. Anthony Tyeeme Clark See page 25.

Carol Moseley Braun

George Rogers Clark (1752–1818) was an American Revolution hero who captured several British forts in the Illinois country.

Hillary Rodham Clinton (1947–) is a former first lady of the United States who was elected as U.S. senator from New York in 2000. Clinton was born in Chicago and grew up in Park Ridge.

Esmé Raji Codell (1968–) is a Chicago teacher and author. Her first book, *Educating Esmé: Diary of a Teacher's First Year*, tells about her experiences as a public school teacher. And her books for young people are often set in Chicago.

Richard J. Daley See page 63.

Richard M. Daley (1942–) followed in the footsteps of his father, Richard J. Daley. He was elected mayor of Chicago in 1989 and was reelected to his sixth term in 2007.

John Deere See page 112.

Stephen Douglas (1813–1861) was an Illinois politician who represented the state in the U.S. Senate for 14 years and held a series of famous debates in 1858 with Abraham Lincoln.

Katherine Dunham (1909–2006) was a dancer who introduced African and African American music and folktales to a wide audience.

Jean-Baptiste Pointe du Sable See page 36.

Ninian Edwards See page 86.

Stephen Douglas

Rahm Emanuel (1959–) is a member of the U.S. House of Representatives from Chicago. In 2006, he helped the Democrats gain control of the House for the first time in 12 years.

Marshall Field (1834–1906) was a Chicago merchant who built the world's largest department store. He was famous for stressing customer service.

Betty Friedan (1921–2006) was a writer and a leader of the feminist movement, the effort to give women equal rights. Her most famous book was *The Feminine Mystique*, published in 1963.

Ulysses S. Grant See page 88.

Luis Gutierrez (1953–) is a Chicago native who got involved with local politics. In 1992, he was elected to the U.S. House of Representatives, the first Latino from the Midwest to serve there.

Alice Hamilton (1869–1970) was a doctor who worked at Chicago's Hull-House and taught at Northwestern University. Her efforts in Illinois led to improvements in public health.

Ernest Hemingway (1899–1961) was a noted author who was born in Oak Park. He won the 1953 Pulitzer Prize for his book *The Old Man and the Sea*.

Mae Jemison (1956–) was the first female African American astronaut. Trained as a doctor, she flew on the space shuttle *Endeavour* in 1992.

Hillary Rodham Clinton

John Johnson (1918–2005) was the founder of the Chicago-based company that publishes *Ebony* and *Jet*, the most successful African American magazines ever.

Robert L. Johnson (1946–) is the founder of Black Entertainment Television and the first African American billionaire. He grew up in Freeport.

Louis Jolliet (1645–1700) was a French Canadian explorer and fur trapper who, in 1673, led the first European expedition into Illinois.

Quincy Jones (1933–) is a jazz and popular music composer known for writing music for films and television. He has won more than two dozen Grammys, the awards given to top recording artists.

Michael Jordan See page 78.

Jackie Joyner-Kersee (1962–) is a track-and-field star from East St. Louis. She has won six Olympic medals.

Percy Julian (1899–1975) was a Chicago researcher who found new uses for soybeans. Some of his greatest successes were synthetic hormones and cortisone.

Abraham Lincoln See page 88.

Elijah Lovejoy See page 47.

Jacques Marquette See page 29.

Cyrus McCormick (1809–1884) invented a reaping machine that made it easier for farmers to harvest wheat. McCormick set up a factory in Chicago to make his reapers.

Frank and Lucy McWorter See page 45.

Bill Murray See page 77.

Stephanie Neely (1963–) has a mind for money. She was named Chicago's city treasurer in 2006.

Barack Obama See page 85.

Linda Sue Park (1960–) is a children's author who explores Korean culture in her work. She won the 2002 Newbery Medal for her book *A Single Shard*.

Richard Peck (1934–) is an author who was born and raised in Decatur. His books are often set in Illinois. He won the 2001 Newbery Medal for *A Year Down Yonder*.

Manuel Perez Jr. See page 60.

Richard Pryor (1940–2005) was a stand-up comedian and actor who addressed racial issues in his work.

George Pullman (1831–1897) invented a luxurious sleeper car that gave train travelers a comfortable ride on long trips. He also founded a factory and a town bearing his name just south of Chicago.

Harold Ramis (1944–) is an actor, film director, and writer. Some of his best-known movies are *Ghostbusters* and *Caddyshack*. He was born in Chicago.

Ronald Wilson Reagan See page 88.

Marie Rouensa (1677–1725) was the daughter of a Kaskaskia leader. She converted to Catholicism and lived in Kaskaskia, where Native Americans and the French got along peacefully.

Carl Sandburg See page 74.

Carol Shields (1935–2003) was the author of the prizewinning novel *The Stone Diaries* and other books. She was born in Oak Park.

Jackie Joyner-Kersee

Shel Silverstein (1930–1999) was a poet, songwriter, musician, cartoonist, and author of children's books. Some of his best-known books are *Where the Sidewalk Ends*, *A Light in the Attic*, *Falling Up*, and *The Giving Tree*. He was born and raised in Chicago.

Louis Sullivan (1856–1924) was a Chicago architect who helped design some of the city's first skyscrapers.

Gustavus Swift (1839–1903) was a Chicago businessman who created an automated system to butcher hogs and cattle. He also introduced a refrigerated railroad car to carry packaged meat across the United States.

James R. Thompson (1936–) was the governor of Illinois from 1976 to 1990—the longest term of service in state history.

Henri de Tonti (1650–1704) was an Italian explorer and trader who, while working for the French, built a trading post in Illinois and helped develop the fur trade there.

Harold Washington See page 64.

Muddy Waters (1915–1983) was a blues singer and guitarist whose real name was McKinley Morganfield. He helped develop the modern electric blues that later shaped many rock musicians.

Ida B. Wells-Barnett (1862–1931) was a journalist who wrote about the horrors of lynchings and other injustices faced by African Americans.

Kanye West (1977–) is a Grammy Award–winning record producer and rap artist. He was born in Chicago.

Ida B. Wells-Barnett

Oprah Winfrey See page 103.

Frank Lloyd Wright (1867–1959) was one of the world's greatest architects who perfected the Prairie style of architecture. He worked with Louis Sullivan before setting off on his own.

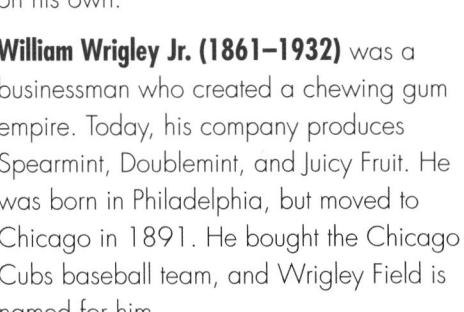

Louis Sullivan

William Wrigley Jr. (1861–1932) was a businessman who created a chewing gum empire. Today, his company produces Spearmint, Doublemint, and Juicy Fruit. He was born in Philadelphia, but moved to Chicago in 1891. He bought the Chicago Cubs baseball team, and Wrigley Field is named for him.

Shan Zhou (1952–) and **Da Huang Zhou (1957–)** were born in China, but moved to Chicago after a visit in 1986. They are known for their huge sculptures and paintings, some of which are seen throughout the city.

Kanye West

RESOURCES

BOOKS

Nonfiction

Brill, Marlene Targ. *Illinois*. 2nd ed. New York: Benchmark Books, 2006.

Holzer, Harold, ed. *Abraham Lincoln, the Writer: A Treasury of His Greatest Speeches and Letters*. Honesdale, Pa.: Boyds Mills Press, 2000.

Kay, Betty Carlson. *Illinois from A to Z*. Urbana: University of Illinois Press, 2000.

Larkin, Tanya. *Jacques Marquette and Louis Jolliet: Explorers of the Mississippi*. New York: Rosen Central, 2004.

Nobleman, Marc Tyler. *Chicago*. Milwaukee, Wis.: World Almanac Library, 2005.

Santella, Andrew. *People of Illinois*. Chicago: Heinemann Library, 2003.

Sutton, Robert P., ed. *The Prairie State: A Documentary History of Illinois, Colonial Years to 1860*. Grand Rapids, Mich.: William B. Eerdmans, 1981.

Sutton, Robert P., ed. *The Prairie State: A Documentary History of Illinois, Civil War to the Present*. Grand Rapids, Mich.: William B. Eerdmans, 1981.

Fiction

Balliett, Blue. *Chasing Vermeer*. New York: Scholastic Press, 2004.

Balliett, Blue. *The Wright 3*. New York: Scholastic Press, 2006.

Cisneros, Sandra. *The House on Mango Street*. New York: A. A. Knopf, 1994.

Codell, Esmé Raji. *Sahara Special*. New York: Hyperion, 2003.

Dell, Pamela. *Liam's Watch: A Strange Story of the Great Chicago Fire*. Excelsior, Minn.: Tradition Books, 2003.

Peck, Richard. *Fair Weather*. New York: Dial, 2001.

Peck, Richard. *A Long Way from Chicago*. New York: Dial, 1998.

Peck, Richard. *A Year Down Yonder*. New York: Dial, 2000.

Robinet, Harriette. *Children of the Fire*. New York: Atheneum, 1991.

DVDs

America's Castles: Windy City Estates. A&E Home Video, 2006.

Chicago Bulls: The 1990s (NBA Dynasty Series). Warner Home Video, 2004.

Chicago: City of the Century. PBS Paramount, 2004.

EXPO: Magic of the White City. Inecom Entertainment Company, 2005.

The Field Museum: Earthly Treasures. Cambridge Educational, 2006.

Forever Loyal: A Salute to the Cubs Fans and Their Field. MPI Home Video, 2003.

Illinois (Discoveries . . . America). Bennett-Watt Entertainment, 2004.

Illinois State Parks (Lee's Visual Guide). Woodchuck Productions, 2004.

Sears Tower. The History Channel, 2007.

Wrigley Field: Beyond the Ivy. Bouganville Productions, 2001.

Young Lincoln: The Early Life of Abraham Lincoln, 1816–1830. FYI Productions, 2005.

WEB SITES AND ORGANIZATIONS

Abraham Lincoln Historical Digitization Project
http:// lincoln. lib.niu.edu/
For historical information about Lincoln's Illinois years

African Americans in Illinois
www.illinoishistory.gov/lib/AfAmHist.htm
To learn more about how black Americans contributed to the state

The Chicago Public Library Digital Collections
www.chipublib.org/digital/digital.html
A unique collection of state history

Digital Past
www.digitalpast.org/nsls.php
Collections from Illinois's cultural institutions, offering historical details about the state

Illinois Alive!
http://history.alliancelibrarysystem.com/IllinoisAlive/index.cfm
To learn more about Illinois's past

Illinois Bureau of Tourism
www.enjoyillinois.com/
To find great places to visit

Illinois Historic Preservation Agency
www.illinoishistory.gov/hs/sites.htm
For more information about the state's historical places

State of Illinois
www.illinois.gov/default.cfm
To learn about the state government

INDEX

★ ★ ★

AUTHOR'S TIPS AND SOURCE NOTES

★ ★ ★

I spent my whole life in New England until 2004, when I moved to Illinois, and now I wonder what took me so long! My new hometown of Chicago is filled with friendly people and amazing sites—along with several libraries where I did research for this book. Some of the most important books I found included *The Prairie State*, a two-volume collection of the writings of Illinoisans from the past; *Frontier Illinois*, by James E. Davis; and Roger Biles's *Illinois*, the most recent, thorough history of the state. Conversations and e-mail exchanges with longtime residents also helped fill in some of the gaps in my Illinois knowledge, along with Web sites maintained by the state of Illinois, local businesses, and nonprofit groups.

Writing *Illinois* for the America the Beautiful series also gave me an excuse to see more of the state for myself. A trip south took me to Springfield and its historic sites, and then to Cahokia, site of the impressive Indian mounds. Along the way, I saw the farmlands that make Illinois a top agricultural producer, and met some of the people who live downstate. A trip west took me to Galena and the rolling hills of the northwest corner, a beautiful spot so different from the bustling city I had left behind. And on these and other trips, I saw the many other towns and cities that make Illinois so diverse.